ONCE OVER LIGHTLY

ONCE OVER LIGHTLY

Written and Illustrated
by Guernsey Le Pelley

Compiled and Edited
by Janet Bassemir

This book was designed by Yellow Inc., Needham, Massachusetts.

It was typeset in Futura Extra Black Condensed and Garamond Light Condensed by dnh typesetting, inc., Cambridge, Massachusetts.

It was printed and bound in the U.S.A. by Bawden Printing, Inc., Eldridge, Iowa.

The articles in this book originally ran in *The Christian Science Monitor*.

ISBN 0-87510-200-X

CONTENTS

AN INTRODUCTION OR IT BEGAN WITH GOVERNOR CURLEY

Opportunity knocks but once, according to one unknown ancient wag, who didn't know beans.

Maybe opportunity knocks only once for some people, but for others it not only knocks more than once, it kicks the door down if they don't answer right away.

What I mean to say is, there are those who start making pizza in their kitchen and in six months they have a chain of pizza parlors all across the United States which are eventually bought up by Pepsi Cola for millions of dollars. Or, someone we can call Mrs. Paul, makes a few crab cakes for her friends and in no time sells the whole kit and kaboodle to Campbell Soup for millions, or maybe billions.

Success never overwhelmed me this way. My definition of success was falling down the cellar stairs and not getting hurt. And it's a wonder opportunity didn't get bored with me because every time it knocked on my door it tripped over the welcome mat.

Once, on my first newspaper job I was mistaken for a bank robber instead of a reporter. Another job I had was selling popcorn on the corner of Hollywood and Vine, a business which did not grow into a national chain of popcorn stands. Instead, on only my second day, a car pulled up to the curb and men with badges got out and started to arrest me for innocently saying, "Get your hot buttered popcorn!" The popcorn, alas, was slathered in coconut oil and the Pure Food Administration took a dim view of calling it butter. I was saved in the nick of time, however, because one of my customers was actor Edward Everett Horton, who put in a good word for me.

Then there was the time I wrote a radio show for WFAA, Dallas, called "Dan Dunn, Secret Operative Number 48" taken from a comic strip. The show nearly came to an untimely end when the sound man pushed a pile of crates over on me to simulate a car crash I had written into the script. I don't remember how long I lay on the floor under boxes of scrap iron and old hub caps, but they tell me I read the last lines on the floor with my head bandaged.

When I finally decided I only wanted to work for a newspaper, opportunity did not give up. I went to Boston. As a freelancer I began selling items to *The Christian Science Monitor*. I set myself up in an apartment furnished in early Salvation Army. I ate at an establishment known as Hayes Bickford, where one could eat for 30 cents if he didn't care what.

I sold enough to the *Monitor* to keep going till one day opportunity went bananas and knocked again. When Gov. Ely lost the election for a second term as governor to James M. Curley it was made-to-order for an out-of-work journalist. I borrowed a press pass and went down to the hotel near the State House where Gov. Elect Curley had his headquarters, hoping to sketch a cartoon of him.

The press pass was useless. Reporters and photographers were roped off and no one was getting close to Curley, who was headed for an upstairs suite for a strategy conference. The former governor had tried to tie up the Curley Administration with a lot of last minute appointees and the damage had to be corrected.

While the guards were distracted I ducked under the ropes and hunched along with a group of aides following Curley to the elevators. I remember wishing I looked more like an Irishman and less like a young, starving, unemployed cartoonist.

I stumbled along with the group into the elevator and we spilled out onto an upper floor and into a large, noisy suite. I perched on a table at one end of the room with my pad and pencil. Curley wasn't far away but there was so much cigar smoke in the room it was hard to see. Besides, I was getting nervous.

For three or four minutes things went just fine. Then suddenly all went quiet.

"Who the blankety-blank is that blankety-blank in the corner?" yelled the Gov. Elect, leveling a finger.

He didn't actually say blankety-blank, of course, but I knew he was talking about me even though I didn't understand the language.

He turned to an aide. "Get a cop up here!" I understood that.

Visions of my near arrests in the past for the hot buttered popcorn and once being mistaken for a bank robber spurred me to action.

"Governor, I'm only trying to draw a picture of you to sell to *The Christian Science Monitor*," I said. For some reason this brought a burst of uncontrollable laughter from one politico which broke the tension. Curley took the unfinished picture and looked at it. "They might not know it's me," he said.

"They will if you sign it," I answered.

Then followed what writers call a pregnant pause. Curley took a pen from an aide's pocket and signed the drawing just as the police entered the room. Then I was helped towards the door, my feet hardly touching the floor because of the firm grip on the seat of my pants. But when we got to the elevators, the policeman said, "OK, lad. Beat it."

The Christian Science Monitor bought the picture. They didn't pay extra for the signature but they put it on the front page (01/03/35). Later the same day I managed to get a sketch of former Gov. Ely, which was also signed. I was then suddenly put on the payroll. The *Monitor*, in its wisdom, saw it could get pictures cheaper if I was on the payroll than if they bought them one by one.

Editor Roscoe Drummond shook my hand and asked me how I liked working for the *Monitor*. I told him it was better than going to jail.

So that's the way Gov. Curley and I got started.

Gov. Curley went on to his destinations.

I went on to mine.

—*Guernsey Le Pelley*

LOVABLE CRITTERS

RACCOONTEUR

According to a very reliable source, raccoons are taking over Scarsdale, N.Y.

This may be long overdue. According to one Old Lyme commuter who wishes to have his name withheld, it is the best news since Coolidge refused to run for a second term. "We have watched Scarsdale over the years," he said, looking out the window of his commuter train, "and frankly, we have never seen a place better suited to raccoons."

Part of the problem stems from the fact that all Scarsdale houses are hidden by trees. And also the highway superintendent is a man by the name of Woodcock. All of which no doubt gives raccoons the impression that if people live in forests and have an official named Woodcock, they also want wildlife. It is a mistaken concept, of course, as birds and other friendly woodland animals have found out.

Evidently, when night comes, Scarsdalians are kept awake by the crashing garbage can lids. As they sit behind barricaded doors they realize they are losing the final battle which will prove raccoons are smarter than people. An issue which has been debated for many generations.

Putting rocks on top of garbage cans has not helped. Several people have even fastened the lids down with chains and padlocks, but, according to statements made in secret council, the raccoons have been able to pick the locks. Either that, or someone is supplying them with keys.

In this computer age, people may be given too much credit for intelligence. This is usually based on such incidental information as that clever Connecticut commuters are using Connecticut Turnpike tokens in place of the more expensive New York subway tokens in the underground turnstiles of Manhattan. But, while this proves a sort of ingenious crookedness on the part of persons whose larcenous ancestors carved wooden nutmegs, it does not say much for the intellect of the billion-dollar subway planners.

In desperation, suggestions have been made to increase the Scarsdale dog population. Fortunately this has been rejected.

Eventually people can learn to coexist with raccoons. It is quite another matter when a community goes to the dogs.

A BIRD'S- AND FROG'S-EYE VIEW

Last week a friend of mine came out of the optometrist's office looking as if he had just spent 10 days on a raft. "I sure haven't got the eyes of an eagle anymore," he said. Of course, he never did have the eyes of an eagle.

Birds, in general, have better eyes than people. On the other hand, people see better than frogs, which should be some consolation.

Frogs, according to my haphazard research, see clearly for only a few inches, which is about the distance for zapping a bug with its tongue. When I was a boy I had a frog for a pet, but it wasn't what you'd call a close relationship. Spoticus was never able to recognize me from anyone else. He could tell I wasn't a fly, but never showed any real affection when I visited him in his screened habitat. He just blinked his big, soporific eyes.

Although Spoticus finally went off one day on his own when someone left the screen open, I still think sightwise he was hit or miss. When we would play together he would often crash into something like a cereal box at the end of a three-foot jump.

Compared with that of frogs and people, the vision of birds is truly amazing. The sharp eagle vision is well known, but I am also impressed with pelicans. We have a pelican friend that visits us once in a while and I know he sees pretty well. Maybe not as well as an osprey, but who wants to quibble?

This pelican (whom we named Rollo) can recognize my wife in the backyard when flying over with a flock of his friends. He will leave the others and circle down to land at my wife's feet for a pat on the head.

Now, I could never tell which pelican was which while they were flying overhead, so it is quite evident to me that birds see better than I do. Still, I'm happy the way things are. I wouldn't want to spend my life diving from 300 feet, smacking the water face-first, just to try to catch a fish in my mouth.

It might prove I had remarkable eyesight, but I am perfectly content to see better than frogs.

BUG OFF

IT SEEMS WE ARE HEADED FOR SUPERBUG. NOTHING KILLS IT, NOTHING FAZES IT

We have gone through the experience of Superman; then we had a period of Superwoman; now it seems we are headed for Superbug.

I have seen enough Sci-Fi and horror movies to know how these things start. In most films some kind of nuclear explosion occurs near an anthill or spider's nest and a mutation takes place. This results in some spiders, or garbage bugs, or whatever, growing to outrageous proportions and attacking some quiet, unassuming city like Toledo, Ohio. Toward the end of the film someone gets the idea to call out the Army and, after a rather unconvincing special effects battle, the bugs are defeated and civilization is saved.

Now it is happening in real life.

While the United States is busy building B-1 bombers, it is being attacked from the rear by superbugs, or "monster bugs" as they are called, which have developed from misuse of insecticides. Superbugs are not only immune from bug sprays but are also free of natural predators according to studies by special agencies.

The main source of dismay is the Asian cockroach. Nothing kills it. Nothing fazes it. Scientists have been too absorbed in defending the US with star wars to notice anything like invading cockroaches, so the Asian cockroach (which also flies) keeps on spreading.

Asia has already invaded the US with cameras, TVs, radios, clothes, computers, and automobiles, all of which seem to be built better than the US product. Now comes a cockroach which is built better than the US version.

So far the US has been unable to come up with any kind of repellent—economically, geopolitically, or entomologically. The national debt goes on; the lack of national control goes on; a confusion as to national policy goes on. And cockroaches go on. Obviously, the modern American needs a new kind of chemistry.

THE PAWS POPULATION

According to recent surveys that give no absolute assurance of accuracy, there are now more cats than dogs in the United States. Populationwise, cats have been gaining on dogs for a number of years and absolutely nothing is being done about it.

Because of this crisis, I attempted to get some pertinent reactions from dog owners as to where they thought America was headed—since it obviously isn't going to the dogs. Opinions from dog people were disappointing. They didn't feel threatened by the cat population, and about 98 percent of them said they didn't think dogs cared one way or the other.

When asked if they thought this would affect the "man's best friend" status of dogs, the answer was almost completely negative, except for one ambiguous reply from a Pomeranian owner who apparently thought he owned a cat.

As one dog family reported, "The dog domain will remain uncorrupted." Dogs will continue to fetch slippers and daily papers, guard property, trace fugitives, sniff out drugs, and the like. One need not worry about Seeing Eye cats, or cats who would nudge deaf people when someone rang the doorbell.

Even confirmed cat owners did not feel that the dog's place in the entertainment industry was seriously threatened. Dogs would not lose traditional leading roles. In other words, it is fairly certain that there will be no cat equivalent of Rin Tin Tin, Lassie, or Benji.

There is, of course, the cartoon cat, Sylvester, but it is said that real cats do not identify with this character.

But the emerging fact remains, cats have, in some subtle manner, become more popular. One can see this not only in the increased, and perhaps illegal, cat population, but in the sales of the greeting card business. The majority of cards, whether Mother's Day cards, birthday cards, or new baby announcements, picture kittens rather than dogs or puppies.

Kittens win the "cute" contest paws down.

KANGAROO CUTE

It is probably not very important in these days of Mideast conflict and East-West nuclear confrontation, but there has been a news item announcing kangaroos are off the endangered species list.

People are still on it, but kangaroos are off. They had been only a hop, skip, and a jump from extinction. They are not totally out of danger. But the kangaroo population is said to be stabilized.

IT IS EASY TO SEE HOW THIS IDEA OF CARRYING THINGS AROUND IN A KANGAROO SKIN BEGAN. THE KANGAROO INVENTED IT.

This means that either people are eliminating fewer kangaroos, or more are being born. Or it could indicate that either people or kangaroos are getting smarter.

The kangaroo got off to a bad start with people, because kangaroo skin is very popular for handbags, suitcases, and golf bags. It is easy to see how this idea of carrying things around in a kangaroo skin began. The kangaroo invented it. One could say the animal has only itself to blame.

The case for kangaroos is something like that for baby seals, beavers, and birds with pretty feathers. If they all weren't so cute and lovable, people wouldn't endanger them. By contrast, sharks aren't on the endangered list. They are too ugly.

Kangaroos have always been a borderline case as far as cuteness goes, and no doubt that is why saving them is suddenly possible.

It now seems quite plausible that, for the sake of whatever kangaroos are left, golf clubs could be carried in another kind of pouch. Either that, or leave the kangaroos alive and train them as caddies.

In addition, kangaroos might even be able to drive golf carts. But one has to be careful. It wouldn't do, for instance, to have them learn to play golf. They would tend to get uppity.

And that would put them right back on the list again.

THE UNHUGGABLE BLACK RHINO

The black rhino is in trouble again. This time it is deep trouble. He has only a couple of years left.

This is a sad case, because no one feels close to a rhinoceros, especially a black rhinoceros. As one fellow down at the tennis courts said, "What have rhinoceroses ever done for me?" People love pandas, whales, eagles, and whooping cranes, but just mention the black rhinoceros and it's a case of "Ho-hum, I'm late for dinner."

The black rhino does not seem huggable. Pandas do, and someone is hugging or kissing Shamu, the killer whale down at Sea World, all the time. One can salute an eagle. If the black rhino is to be saved, it must be presented as cute, if not downright cuddly, but alas, it has a face only a mother could love. Even with a mother, it's a borderline case. Without a doubt, the black rhino is the ugliest creature since the triceratops—unless one counts the malicious poachers who murder the species.

Certain zoologists say the black rhino never hurt anyone. It is a sweet and caring animal even if it does look like something time forgot. What makes its case especially difficult is that dealers in rhino parts consider the animal worth more dead than alive. A rhino horn dagger sells for $15,000, and the horn, powdered, brings $5,000 a pound in Middle Eastern drugstores. Actually, preserving the animals would bring more profits to those regions in Africa where they are still found, since tourism brings more money in the long run.

I have never even seen a black rhino, and none of my friends have ever seen one, but I think the world should have them. Probably the black rhino thinks so, too.

Whenever I mention that it would be nice to save the black rhino from extinction, people say there are more worthwhile things we should be doing—like feeding the hungry in one's cities close to home. Well, it is hard to argue with that. I'm for feeding hungry people.

I suspect, though, after the last black rhino has been killed off for profit a few years from now, that people will still be hungry. Maybe even hungrier, since "not caring" can always hide behind some excuse.

NO NEWTS IS GOOD NEWTS

Fortunately for all of us, the arms race and rising budgets aren't the only things in the news coming out of Washington. There are other things, slightly less troubling, but more bewildering, and we are not referring to speeches made by the President.

IT HAS BEEN DISCOVERED THAT WASHINGTON IS FULL OF NEWTS AND FROGS

Bewildering information also comes from the Smithsonian.

After some sort of survey, made for obscure reasons, it has been discovered that Washington is full of newts and frogs. At first this was believed to be propaganda put out by the Democrats, but it does have a basis in fact. The information may have been put out simply in the belief it would give Americans, if not the world, a nicer picture of Washington. Maybe wholesome is the word.

But according to Lightly's unofficial survey, newts and frogs have an opposite effect. According to findings, they give people the shudders and screaming meemees. Anyone who has seen any horror movies at all knows that when you get to a place full of newts and frogs, you are only one step away from the damp dungeon where the monster lives.

Of course, there are also snakes.

The news reassures us that the only dangerous snake found in Washington is the copperhead. This source didn't specify in which part of Washington the snakes are located, but it didn't exclude the corridors of Congress.

To find there are newts, frogs, and copperheads in the capital is not surprising when one considers all the other things that are going on. The copperhead has been there since the Civil War and is considered sneaky and extremely unobliging since it doesn't rattle before it bites you the way a rattlesnake does. People in the North who sided with the South were called copperheads. This sneakiness is not necessarily limited only to snakes found in the capital.

The question rises from time to time, why the snakes are not driven out of Washington. It is not an easy job. Usually they are sent there from other places.

OINK!

Some people watch the morning news on television for trends in society; others read editorials or just the headlines, or even Evans and Novak. For our part, we watch bumper stickers.

Anyone who has been watching bumper stickers as we have will be aware that pigs have risen to first place in the affections of Americans. And it's about time. Typical examples of the pig's progress on bumpers are: "Have you hugged your pig today?" or "Honk if you love pigs."

For too long the pig has been the despised term of bitterest opprobrium. But as is often the case in vicious unfairness, the object of hate has dissolved its unpleasant bonds by the sheer injustice of the attack.

We spoke to a male chauvinist pig of our acquaintance a few days ago and found him in high spirits. He had always been a delightful person and we were glad to know he had not suffered unduly. He was as pleased with his new rise in status as he had been sad when pigs were scorned.

"I did think it was terribly unfair," he mused, "to praise chauvinist women as liberators while chauvinist men were called pigs. But it's all right now that pigs are lovable."

Later on we interviewed a policeman as to how he liked his designation as pig. "Oh, it's not bad. As a pig, I feel I have come up in the world. Pigs are people, too, you know."

Pig pictures and dolls are everywhere. Recently in a gift shop I encountered a kindly lady buying a huge stuffed pig. She smiled. "Last year I bought my granddaughter a stuffed cat, the year before it was a dog, and the year before that it was a bear. So I'm not allowed to buy her any more animals. This year I can keep the pig for myself."

The wonderful thing about this year of the pig is that it proves nothing stays on the bottom forever. Everyone can hope.

Even if you are one of those people who get called names like chicken, snake-in-the-grass, shrimp, or even a worm, one day you are sure to gain a rise in status. An animal-lover friend of ours thinks the time is coming when the rat will be better thought of.

Just yesterday, as I was about to cross the street with permission of the "walk" light, I did not see a car full of kids make a speeding right turn at the intersection. The one in the seat nearest me yelled, "Watch where you're going, you old buzzard!"

As a buzzard, I patiently await my time of ascendancy.

MYTHICAL CREATURES: UNICORNS AND BUSYBODIES

Everyone who reads a newspaper or watches TV has been aware of the return of the legendary unicorn. It has been discovered by those intrepid explorers who search the fringes of our childhood, Barnum and Bailey.

The glory lasted only a few days before the Busybodies began their relentless campaign against the wrongdoers of the world. I'm not in favor of wrongdoers. It is just the charred smell of vengeance I deplore.

Unfortunately, there is this Busybody element in the United States, which sits breathing heavily in our midst, ready to pounce upon anything that moves sideways. They can be recognized by the spots of paint on their clothes (which never dries) from the endless painting of picket signs. Their voices are slightly hoarse from shouting, "End the . . ." or "Down with . . ."

Although their cause is eminently just, I feel they seethe and hiss too much, and are too unaware of how unacceptably somber an instant Utopia would be.

But now, because of these Busybodies, experts have been called in. It was not quite the Supreme Court, but they were impressively grim. So, after much ado, Barnum and Bailey's little unicorn was coerced into a humiliating public examination. Although the world was not exactly rocked with surprise, the unicorn turned out to be a goat. A one-horned goat —but still, a goat.

I grieve about this.

Of course, I knew it was a goat. And all the players down at the town tennis courts knew it was a goat. But alas, Barnum and Bailey's goat didn't know he was a goat. Up until the self-righteous Busybodies descended upon him he thought he was a princely unicorn. Now he looks out at a computer-smart public in shame. Now he has no more dreams.

Couldn't wrongdoers be more gently educated in the Busybody's strict code of ethics? While it is true they are always right, I just wish they would politely ring the doorbell at Utopia's gate instead of always battering down the doors.

Unicorn, take heart. We love you.

FRIENDLY MOSQUITOES

WHILE THERE IS NO PROOF THAT FLORIDA MOSQUITOES CARRY OFF CHILDREN, ALLIGATORS, AND SMALL MOBILE HOMES, THEY HAVE FEARSOME REPUTATIONS

The Florida mosquito isn't as big as the New Jersey mosquito (it takes only six New Jersey mosquitoes to carry off a full-grown man and dump him in the swamps), but Florida mosquitoes are small and mean. While there is no proof that Florida mosquitoes carry off children, alligators, and small mobile homes, they have fearsome reputations and are known for their poor dispositions.

But according to certain biological laboratories, there is a new mosquito in Florida, friendly to Floridians. This new mosquito holds no grudges against people and doesn't bite them. The study came about because it no longer does any good to spray for the common Florida mosquito. They have become immune to chemical insecticides, and many believe they thrive on them. The answer seems to be to stop spraying chemicals and support the big, green, people-loving mosquito. One of its chief claims to fame is that it likes to eat the small, mean, people-biting mosquito. In fact it seems that even the larvae of this new mosquito like to eat the larvae of the mean, old, people-biting mosquito. So, the theory goes, eventually there will be only the big, happy, friendly green mosquitoes left.

So far this experiment is being conducted on a small scale, and there has been no noticeable change in the mosquito population. Larger experiments are being planned, however, and the results will be carefully studied. No serious problems are as yet seen.

Except maybe one. Don't swat the *Toxorhynchites splendens.*

He is your friend.

THAT'S HERBERT'S
PET ALLIGATOR ~
WHERE'S
HERBERT
?

SMILEY 'GATORS

AN ALLIGATOR'S HEAD IS NOT IDEAL FOR PETTING, BEING SOMEWHAT LIKE THE SIDE OF A RAW PINEAPPLE

Most places in the United States if a person says he owns a pet, one assumes it is either a dog or a cat. This does not necessarily hold true in Florida, where pets and owners seldom fit the norm.

It is possible a native Floridian would recognize a dog or cat if he saw one, but in all likelihood he would be a resident of Miami or Boca Raton.

If complaints in newspapers and on TV are any guide, the typical Florida pet is either a goat or some giant bird that swears. Apparently the complaints about goats have some foundation in fact, since there are stories of goats boosting an old codger into the creek now and then. And one elderly gentleman complained that just the smell of his neighbor's goat keeps his wife awake all night.

Smells, however, are not against the law in Florida. As it turns out, goats, chickens, cows, pigs, and the like are OK to have around the yard. You get goat, pig, and chicken mixed with night-blooming jasmine or honeysuckle and you can understand why Scarlett O'Hara was so irascible.

Among the other animals found around Florida houses are lions, small elephants, and small various snakes. Several otherwise pleasant families keep banana spiders. A banana spider is not the usual dime-sized arachnid that wobbles into view appearing to be underfed. Banana spiders are closer to the size of small baseball mits and are yellow and black like warning signs on the highway. These spiders have no special qualities of affection the way a dog has, but if not downright friendly they are at least neutral. Their chief attraction is that they eat cockroaches (known here as palmetto bugs).

Occasionally in Florida an alligator is discovered as someone's pet. On TV recently a fellow in a sports shirt held an eight-footer in his lap, stroking it affectionately on the head. An alligator's head is not ideal for petting, being somewhat like the side of a raw pineapple, but the alligator blinked quietly and seemed to be smiling. For what reason he was smiling I could not be sure.

The man maintained that the neighborhood had not complained about Gorbachev (the alligator's name) in any way, since the population on the street has remained stable and no one has reported any missing family members.

IF YOU'RE A DOG, LET ME HEAR YOU BARK !

GOING TO THE DOGS

Nobody talks about "dog days" anymore.

When I was a kid, dog days was a season to go through just like Thanksgiving and Christmas. At the arrival of July and August some ghoulish busybody would always mention the fact that "we should take it easy because we were going into dog days!"

The very words had an ominous sound, and I remember having an uneasy feeling that I should be looking over my shoulder in case I was being attacked by some giant Hound of the Baskervilles crazy with the heat. The mystic words gave July and August, which might otherwise be just hot and boring, a macabre excitement. Even the heat waves shimmering up off the pavements issued a warning of unknown adventure.

But despite all the warnings, the neighborhood dogs didn't seem to care what month it was. They loafed around apparently unaware of their seasonal obligation for menace.

Yet it was still a few years before I discovered that dog days didn't have anything to do with dogs, per se. The term dog days, I discovered, comes from the fact that during July and August, Sirius, the brightest star in the constellation Canis Major, rises and sets with the sun. Sirius, being part of Canis Major, is called the "dog star." The same thing works for Procyon, a bright star in Canis Minor.

So it seems there is no medieval hocus-pocus about dog days. It has all the magic of a vernal equinox or an eclipse of the sun. Discovering this was a sad disappointment, much like the first realization that there wasn't any Santa Claus. In fact it was doubly heartbreaking because it came about at the same time I found out that eating raw carrots didn't really enable me to see in the dark. It is too bad that as one grows older the world becomes more and more prosaic.

Dogs, people, and even cats act differently in a spell of hot weather. Maybe reaction to hot weather gave dog days an added significance. But if this is so, why not call them "people days" or "cat days"?

Well, there are still a few things left such as "Red sky at morning, sailors take warning; red sky at night, sailors' delight." If some hard-nosed meteorologist pulls the plug on this one, I'll be ready to give up on mankind.

FEARLESS LEADERS

GREAT AND NEAR GREAT

There has been a sort of rhubarb going on in the New Hampshire state house over where to hang the portrait of Franklin Pierce. For many years now, some people think he has been hanging too far from George Washington who is more or less front and center, sharing the limelight with that other well-known President, Abraham Lincoln.

Some readers today might not recognize the name Franklin Pierce and thus not know he was President of the United States back in 1853. Of course, a lot of people back in 1853 didn't know he was President either, since he was never very conspicuous.

Apparently Mr. Pierce has been hanging almost in a corner as a ho-hum item for a long time. This is normal for an obscure president. But since Mr. Pierce was the only President New Hampshire can boast of and since he was not such a bad-looking fellow, there is some logical reason to feel he should not be sloughed aside—giving place to someone like Daniel Webster who was neither a president nor handsome.

Whatever stature Franklin Pierce has attained, many think it was the result of being compared with Millard Fillmore, or James Buchanan, who were the Presidents who came before and after. In fact, Pierce might have been a sort of high point in a series of low points like John Tyler, James Polk, and Zachary Taylor, none of whom were likely to move George Washington from stage center.

The crowning prize for obscurity was offered by the Democratic Party in 1857 when they didn't think he was worth renominating. This could be considered a real put-down since Democrats have been renominating losers in significant numbers.

Franklin Pierce managed to fight in the Mexican war without becoming a hero. He did, however, work his way up to being a brigadier general, but it hasn't seemed to impress anyone in New Hampshire.

His cause has recently been taken up by a few prominent New Hampshirites, who believe he is one of the greatly underrated presidents and that he should be right up there along with President Jimmy Carter. The gains have not been spectacular.

As far as we know, Franklin Pierce is still in the corner.

THE PRESIDENCY: APPEARANCE IS EVERYTHING

Someone like James A. Garfield could not be elected president today, even though he was fluent in Greek and Latin and a liberal Republican. He simply could never hack it on television.

Public image and show business now elect presidents. The ritual of making promises in speeches and writing a party platform may still persist as part of the American myth, but it's how the person plays his part on television that gathers votes.

In Richard Nixon's great television debate with John F. Kennedy he had bad makeup advice. His speech, many thought, was better than Mr. Kennedy's, but he lost the election in great part because his "five o'clock shadow" made him look like a member of the Mafia.

I recently overheard a political discussion between two women seated on the bench at the bus stop comparing the merits of the two presidential candidates.

"I don't understand," the lady in the pink pantsuit said, "why every time a poll comes out, fewer and fewer women say they will vote for George Bush. What did George Bush ever do to women?"

"He ain't done nothing to women," the lady in the sleeveless blouse said. "It's just the way he talks. He sounds like a husband."

This brought several moments of silence, while the women, I suppose, were trying to imagine a husband as president. Finally Pink Pantsuit said, "There was Harry Truman. He was a husband type. But it doesn't explain why a larger percent of women are voting for Michael Dukakis. He's awfully short." She held her hand about four feet off the ground. "Besides that, it seems like his head is too heavy. It wobbles when he walks."

The sleeveless blouse lady looked surprised. "I never noticed that!"

"Oh, yes. You just watch him on television when he's walking to meet people. In our family we call him Mr. Heavy Head. He seems to be always walking uphill. A president shouldn't have a wobbly head."

"I never would have voted for Jesse Jackson," said sleeveless blouse.

"Jackson doesn't have a heavy head. He seems light-headed."

"It's not his head," she replied. "It's his thumb. When he does thumbs up his thumb bends too far back. Like a Russian sickle, or the letter C."

At this moment the bus came. The last thing I heard was: "Barbara Bush would make a darling First Lady."

ARE THE CANDIDATES REAL TIMBER?

I DREAMED NOBODY GOT ELECTED PRESIDENT . . . IF THIS HAPPENS THERE WILL HAVE TO BE SOME SORT OF CARETAKER GOVERNMENT WHILE THINGS GET SORTED OUT

Not very long ago I woke up screaming in the middle of the night. Well, it wasn't really the middle of the night, it was more like five a.m. and I wasn't actually screaming. But it was a horrible dream just the same.

I dreamed nobody got elected president.

The problem seemed to be that out of 245 million people in the United States the best presidential candidates that could be found were Michael Dukakis and George Bush. This is a frightening development to many. When I took an unofficial poll as to presidential preference down at the town tennis courts, half the players said, "I'm not voting for Dukakis." The other half said, "I'm not voting for Bush."

I'm not sure what this means. Saying you won't vote for somebody doesn't necessarily mean you will vote for somebody else. When Mr. Bush makes a speech, I notice he doesn't make a strong plea to vote for him. He warns everyone not to vote for Mr. Dukakis. On the other hand, Dukakis tells people not to vote for Bush. There is a rumor going around that during Dukakis' speeches a lot of people fall asleep and on more than one occasion, Dukakis was one of them.

Then there is Jesse Jackson. The Rev. Mr. Jackson always makes the best speeches, if one doesn't press too hard for the meaning of what he says. His main problem with the tennis court group is that he is a black preacher who never got elected to anything, and has been friendly with Fidel Castro and Yasser Arafat in the belief that this passes for foreign policy.

Theoretically, though, Americans are stuck with either Dukakis or Bush. So what is going to happen on election day? No one is going to vote for anybody. If this happens there will have to be some sort of a caretaker government while things get sorted out.

But, good heavens, that might mean House Speaker James Wright would be president, unless the House Ethics Committee removes him. Then (gasp) it would be John Stennis, president pro tem of the Senate—and if he doesn't make it, it falls to George Shultz.

I'm glad I don't know how this is going to turn out.

THE BABY CIRCUIT

IF A PROSPECTIVE CANDIDATE CAN'T SURVIVE 30 OR MORE PRIMARIES ON A DIET OF DRIED HAM SANDWICHES . . . HE FORFEITS THE GAME OR GOES DIRECTLY TO JAIL

As the primary election campaign in the United States gets closer, its faults become more apparent. Perhaps the only thing on the positive side is that it makes TV reruns look better.

This is a time for conditioning oneself. Every four years both the public and the candidates must be in top physical shape. American presidents don't win presidential elections, opponents merely fall by the wayside. Since 1977 this has been called Carteronian Democracy.

The American system works on the same basis as an obstacle course, or even a game of Monopoly. If a prospective candidate can't survive 30 or more primaries on a diet of dried ham sandwiches, or precooked airplane dinners of fricassee of lamb, he forfeits the game or goes directly to jail.

While there is some conditioning to be gained by jogging in the early morning and sleeping in a smoke-filled room at night, there is little a candidate can do to prepare himself for baby kissing. Babies invariably are licking strawberry ice cream cones at kissing time. Some say being able to eat cold farina off someone else's plate is fortifying, and, also, if a candidate likes warm strawberry ice cream to begin with, it gives him a slight edge. But usually kissing babies is just "cold turkey," as the saying goes.

Jimmy Carter was a good example of how, if a man endures to the end, he becomes president. The justice who administered the oath of office allegedly called him "Jimmy What's-his-name." No one knew who Jimmy Carter was. He was just there at the end. But people who drop out along the way become even more unknown. Several, after returning from the hustings, were never recognized even by their own families.

One big problem of the system is that the ability to win a campaign is not necessarily the ability to be president. Along with Jimmy Carter, John F. Kennedy was a prime example of a champion campaigner but a bit short on qualities to govern. So, after he was elected, he just kept on campaigning. It is the next best thing.

We would advocate changing the system, but they say that all this inefficiency and wasteful spending helps the economy.

MARTIN VAN WHO?

Perhaps no one has noticed, but upbeat journalism is the new trend. As a trend it is not overwhelming, and it still does not offset the usual violence and crisis on which the news media thrive, but it is there and should be noticed.

One item which might be classed as upbeat journalism is that Kinderhook, N.Y., has recently decided to honor Martin Van Buren. As far as upbeat goes, Martin Van Buren is a borderline case, but bringing his name into the news has something cheerful about it, and it isn't going to threaten the popularity of the President.

It is recorded somewhere in the town hall that Van Buren was born in Kinderhook. It is just that up until now nobody particularly cared. Maybe Van Buren himself tried to hush it up.

Some think that the reason it took Kinderhook so long to celebrate the fact it is a presidential birthplace is that no one in town knew Martin Van Buren had been president. This isn't peculiar to Kinderhook. A lot of people didn't know it. Evidently, according to some speculation, a few tourists drove through town looking for a monument, and that started the ball rolling.

They found a monument. It was hidden by some weeds, but it was there. From then on there was a hometown movement to make Martin Van Buren a celebrity.

It turned out, unfortunately, that his birthplace had been torn down in 1920. It was considered an eyesore. Since Kinderhook is not widely known as the Athens of America, it must have been an eyesore indeed. Anyway, it is unlikely it was torn down out of spite. In our modern society, memorials are not as important as parking lots.

The Van Buren mansion, in which he later lived, has been cleaned up. His name is recorded on numerous signs. Parades and grand balls are given in his honor. And, while Martin Van Buren's name still doesn't come up often at parties in Washington, these things can change.

PRESIDENTS WITH VICES

IN THE OLD DAYS, ONE VOTED FOR PRESIDENT AND THAT WAS THAT, BUT NOTHING IS SIMPLE ANYMORE

This is the year when Americans will be consciously voting for a vice-president.

In the old days, one voted for president and that was that, but nothing is simple anymore. A few days ago, one of my friends down at the town tennis courts said, "It would be easier to vote for Dukakis if Bentsen were running for president." He may have meant the ticket would work one way as well as another. Or he may have been thinking of how the president would look standing next to Prime Minister Margaret Thatcher.

George Bush tried to clear things up for his running mate in a speech to the veterans. Dan Quayle, he implied, is qualified to be vice-president because he didn't burn the American flag. It makes a clean and simple qualification, but in Senator Quayle's case there always seems to be some confusion between competence and patriotism.

The puzzled public has been told at least 500 times that vice-presidential nominee Quayle looks like Robert Redford. Before the convention, however, no one ever told Mr. Redford he looked like Mr. Quayle. This may mean only that more people go to the movies than visit golf courses.

Quayle at 41 isn't exactly young. He only seems young. What the news media got at the convention was an impression of immaturity. At a time when Quayle should have been scared, overawed, or impressed with the great responsibility being thrust upon him, the first words of his acceptance speech were a vapid "I can see we're going to have a lot of fun in this campaign."

Anyway, there may have been good reason for nearly all of the 13,000 reporters at the Republican convention suddenly circling hapless Quayle. Maybe it is because they thought when Mr. Bush opened his mouth they could believe just exactly what they were getting. When Quayle opened his, nobody could believe it.

LIFE-SIZE PRESIDENTS

There is one small, unresolved problem which patriotic Americans ought to look into. The Smithsonian Institution lacks life-size portraits of four past presidents of the United States.

This same danger has not threatened statues in parks. Not only were life-size statues the going thing in past generations, the artist usually added a horse. Statues of people on horses naturally declined when the automobile came in, and since then it has seemed too gauche to portray the president sitting in the back seat of a gas guzzler.

Big portraits are lacking for the last three Presidents—Ford, Carter, and Reagan. The other one is no less than Thomas Jefferson.

In the face of no full-size portrait of President Jefferson it can be speculated he did not want to spend the money. Spending money was not popular in those days.

But also, he may have deemed it unnecessary, since his portrait would eventually appear on so many nickels, after all the buffaloes were gone.

It is much harder to determine why the last three American Presidents did not have life-size portraits.

As for President Ford, he may not have been in office long enough. It is possible the picture got started but that the artist only got down as far as the second button on his vest, just below the "WIN" button.

When Jerry Ford did not return to Washington after the election, it may have seemed inappropriate to finish the portrait out in California while Jerry was wearing a golf shirt.

As for President Carter, some think a mistake was made. He actually had a full-size portrait painted, but no one realized it. It may have been hung next to President Lincoln, for instance, but didn't seem full length. Another theory is that when he had a full-length portrait painted he was wearing a brown sweater and the Smithsonian didn't want it.

It is the case of President Reagan that is somewhat puzzling. When he was in the movies there were life-size posters all over the front of the theater—playing football, fighting Indians, wooing starlets. It may be that he is trying to have one of these earlier reproductions converted into an official Smithsonian picture.

Or maybe he is working on one bigger than life-size.

THE REAGAN BUST

If anyone has been yearning for a 14-inch porcelain bust of President Reagan for Christmas, his wish can be fulfilled. The bust is done with a cowboy shirt and what should pass for a realistic, movie-likc Technicolor. It sells for $3,000, which proves times are getting better.

This tempting item, as well as other "historic and heirloom quality merchandise," is available in the GOP gift catalog, a 16-page booklet called "The Official Republican Collection." If you have not received one, you are probably on the wrong list.

Prices seem to run a bit high, but with Christmas coming on this is no time to cater to a depressed economy. Undoubtedly there are thousands of people who would like to have a porcelain bust of President Reagan in a cowboy shirt, but who simply do not have a place to put it. Its size of 14 inches makes it too large for a paperweight but too small to go on top of the fountain in the flower garden or at the shallow end of the swimming pool. We measured our birdbath but decided a porcelain Reagan would be inappropriate, since at present we have a cement turtle.

At the time this is written only one porcelain bust has been sold. Maybe it was ordered by someone in the White House, we aren't sure. As far as we know, there is no bust of Nancy, which is too bad because two such items might be more useful. There must be any number of California Republicans who could use some $6,000 bookends. Also there is no bust of the vice-president. Probably people wouldn't know who it was.

There are other, more costly items. A limited edition collection of engraved portraits of all the presidents, bound in leather, sells for $20,000. This would inevitably include some Democratic presidents and since there are 40 presidents in all, one would be paying $500 apiece. That means an engraved Ronald Reagan is going for the same price as a Harry Truman, which boggles the mind; unless, of course, the engraving of Harry Truman could pass for John Wayne.

DATES OF NOTE

What Goes Down . . .

This year being the ninth anniversary of the eruption of Mt. St. Helens, it may be time to bring up a theory about the eruption which is going the rounds down here in Florida and which seems to have been suppressed until now.

It cannot likely be proved one way or the other whether any media plot is involved, but very few people throughout the United States realized what was happening in Florida on the East Coast while Mt. St. Helens was erupting on the West Coast.

Florida was getting sucked under, that's what was happening.

While Mt. St. Helens was blowing stuff into the air out West, in Florida everything was sliding down into sinkholes.

Not many people down at the town tennis courts were affected by this at the time, but one can't help wondering.

All that stuff Mt. St. Helens blew into the air must have come from somewhere.

I don't know too much about the geological theories involved here, but a lot of Florida people out in the middle of the state feel that the whole world might be connected up somewhere underneath.

The issue is coming up anew.

There has been speculation that Mt. St. Helens is going to erupt again, though this time in a much tamer fashion.

As a result a lot of scientific people, mostly with whiskers, are traveling to Washington State to see what's going up.

Not one, that I am aware of, is coming to Florida to see what's going down! That's the pressure of mass opinion for you.

But some Florida farmers I know of are keeping a lonely watch out on the back pastures. Some kind of record should be kept. These people feel they would know for sure if a 1972 Olds that slid into a sinkhole somewhere around Orlando five years ago were to come smoking down a mountainside in the Gifford Pinchot National Forest out in the state of Washington.

I think a class-action suit in the Supreme Court is unlikely. I'm just bringing it up for consideration.

LAYERS OF DELIGHT

Everyone is so full of gloating self-satisfaction and patriotism from celebrating the 100th anniversary of the Statue of Liberty that many may be unaware we are also celebrating the 75th anniversary of the Oreo cookie.

At first blush it may seem there is no comparison between Oreo cookies and the Statue of Liberty, but one must concede that the humble Oreo cookie has played its part in the formation of American society. It is true that for a full generation immigrants had been waving to Miss Liberty before they started eating Oreos, but if marketing experts are to be believed, by 1912 all the immigrants had expanded their expectations of the new country. After they cheered the statue and settled down in their respective ghettos, they rushed out to taste the fruits of freedom, which took the form of countless boxes of Oreos.

Some waggish statistician has estimated that the amount of Oreo cookies eaten by subsequent immigrants—and a few others—would, if piled on top of each other, reach to the moon eight times. For a cookie made in a plain, black and white pattern with no frills, this seems like a tremendous amount.

So it must be reckoned with. Along with the lady holding the torch, one of the great inducements of coming to America was the availability of delectable items such as the Oreo cookie. Although comparisons may be odious, as some poor sports aver, it certainly puts the United States ahead of the Russians with their cabbage soup.

Of course, the Oreo cookie is not without controversy. At one time it was advertised on TV by the famous George Burns, who dipped his Oreo in a glass of milk and then obligingly took a bite of it. The expression on his face could have been described only as being bewildered. It might have been because this was the first Oreo cookie he ever tasted, or that he was not normally a cookie dunker.

I know I certainly am not a dunker. I take the top off my Oreo and eat it first. Then I eat the half with that white creamy stuff, sipping my milk as I do so.

Immigrants have their memories of the first glimpse of the Statue of Liberty, but their children have eaten enough Oreos to reach eight times to the moon. They have memories, too.

A PENNY A PIG, TOO

THE BROOKLYN BRIDGE WAS BUILT NOT SO PEOPLE COULD GET INTO MANHATTAN, BUT SO PEOPLE COULD GET OUT

New Yorkers, who seem to be always celebrating something, recently celebrated the 100th anniversary of the Brooklyn Bridge.

Yankee fans boycotted the ceremony because allegedly they thought that building the bridge was what led to the discovery of Brooklyn.

This isn't exactly true. Brooklyn already was in existence. And if Brooklyn hadn't existed someone would have invented it. The main reason the bridge was built was not so people could get into Manhattan; it was built so people could get out.

Mayor Koch has described the bridge as the eighth wonder of the world. Anything that has withstood New York traffic for 100 years should be rated right up there with the pyramids. The feat seems all the greater when one considers that, unlike almost everything else today, it was built with American steel.

American "public relations" also rates as one of the wonders of the world. For evidence of this, the mention of the Brooklyn Bridge never brings to mind the name of John Roebling, the man who built it, but of Steve Brody, who claimed to have jumped off it. Which he probably didn't. The only thing in those days that rivaled the size of the Brooklyn Bridge was Steve Brody's mouth.

The size of the bridge is, and was, impressive. At the time it was built it was the tallest thing in the city, including Brooklyn. It also had the reputation of being sold more than any other piece of real estate to naive immigrants with a few dollars to spend. Even Boss Tweed sold his shares to some artless person because he believed the bridge would never be finished. He thought he was getting rid of some worthless stock.

But after about 14 years the bridge was finished and it began to make money charging a 1-cent toll for people walking across. It was the same price for a pig. Evidently 1 cent was also considered pretty big in those days.

CANNED IN THE SERVICE

Recently we celebrated the 200th anniversary of the Constitution of the United States and also the 50th anniversary of the Golden Gate Bridge. These lofty happenings have somewhat overshadowed a more modest celebration, the 50th anniversary of canned Spam.

Any veteran of World War II who is still nipping about can well remember the impact Spam had on his life. One could say it was the biggest thing to happen to him that he didn't have to be hospitalized for. He had Spam and eggs (powdered) for breakfast, Spam sandwiches for lunch, and Spam and potatoes (canned or dried) for supper. This evoked a whole series of wisecracks about the product, such as "It was ham that didn't pass the physical."

Of course, Spam wasn't all that bad. The word is a shortened term for "spiced ham," which sounds harmless enough until eaten for about a week. It was never ground up and sold for dog food, as some GIs suggested. I know it was eaten in many ways. One of my buddies always soaked it in his coffee and considered it quite tasty.

After Spam was tried out on the US Army with no ill effects, it was introduced to the Russians, who loved it. I am not sure what it replaced in the Russians' diet, but they said it was great with cabbage. Maybe they said it was great compared with cabbage, I can't recall.

While I was in the Army I dreamed, as did thousands of other GIs, of the delicious home-cooked meals awaiting me when the war was over. The dream and the experience finally came to pass.

I remember rumbling into the house in my Army boots, the scurrying, shouting, laughing, and tears. Finally I remember gathering around the table and the flourish of bringing in a platter of food.

"A wonderful thing happened while you were away," exclaimed my wife. "A new product came on the market, called Spam. I've got some for you to try."

Eventually things calmed down and got straightened out. Now that Spam has endured for 50 years and I have mellowed somewhat, I feel I can enter into the celebration.

GLOBE TROTTING

GERTIE.. GET ME SOME KIND OF STICK!

LETTING THINGS LEAN

Just about every year a new crisis report comes out concerning the Leaning Tower of Pisa. That is, the report is new. It is the same old crisis of leaning over too far.

Generally speaking, the tower manages to lean about .05 of an inch farther each year. Each year certain concerned officials announce that, if something isn't done pretty soon, the whole contraption is going to topple over.

This seems like a reasonable conclusion.

Unfortunately, no one seems really convinced, except those few tourists who stand a safe distance away while taking a snapshot.

This leads us to suggest the Leaning Tower of Pisa is very much like everything else going on in the world.

The tower was built in 1173 and started leaning almost immediately. So, as incredible as it sounds, the 180-foot building has been falling over for at least 800 years and no one has yet figured out what to do about it. If anything.

The fact that this whimsical catastrophe is happening in Italy may give rise to a few Italian jokes, but it is our position the problem is universal.

Not only is there no great stampede to save the structure, no one seems absolutely sure what is going on. According to an AP report, the tower is leaning 16 feet off the perpendicular. According to Webster's New World Dictionary, it is leaning more than 17 feet. According to Architecture of Europe it leans only a mere 13 feet. These are but a few of the authoritative opinions.

Either there is some expert incompetence here, or the tower moves back and forth when no one is looking.

In order that this magnificent structure should not be a total waste, how about putting a sign on it which says: "This tower represents all the problems of Planet Earth." People have become used to simplified symbols, like a graph showing unemployment rise over a decade, or one of those giant thermometers in the town square representing donations to the Firemen's Fund.

The problems it represents might suggest everything from the pollution of Earth's air, soil, and water to the threat of nuclear or non-nuclear war. Like the tower they all seem to lean a little toward collapse each year for want of vigorous solutions.

Of course, there is one vital flaw in using the Leaning Tower as our picture parable. If the tower falls over, there will still be a lot of people standing around. They will be able to shake their heads and say, "What a pity someone didn't do something to save it."

I FOUND THAT ONE SUNSET CARD I SELECTED IN SARASOTA, FLA., WAS MADE IN BUFFALO, N.Y.

Selecting post cards during one's vacation ranks among the great challenges of mankind. It is second only to deciding what to tip a Washington cabdriver who doesn't speak a word of English.

First of all, the picture post cards on the rack never show immediate surroundings.

They are always of distant landmarks one never got to see.

There is a wide selection of sunsets, however. They all have a lavish red quality, suggesting not so much a lovely evening as the end of the world. Also, if you are one who reads the printing, you find that none of the pictures were even taken in the area. I found that one sunset card I selected in Sarasota, Fla., was made in Buffalo, N.Y.

The average person feels doomed in the face of things like this.

Of course, one could write a note on all sunset cards saying, "I have been here a week and so far have never seen a sunset this good."

Usually I try for a card showing the local beach. Now, a typical beach scene would show a stout middle-aged gentleman standing in the surf wearing an ill-fitting pair of flowered shorts and handing his pleasant, round wife the remains of a starfish. One can search every store on the main street but will never find this scene on a post card.

Sometimes I try to find a card showing the flora and fauna. But the nearest thing in Florida is an assortment of alligator pictures. And there is always one of a posed alligator biting a frenzied native in the seat of the pants. It will have a caption something like: "Having my afternoon nip in Florida."

Mostly, I end up taking a free post card from the hotel (which is always a picture of the hotel) and putting an "X" on the window of my room.

My message: "Having great time. Wish you were here. X marks my room."

SKYJACK TO CUBA

There have been a lot of airline hijackings from the United States to Cuba, but apparently no one is counting. Shouldn't something be done about it?

Since American crime in the streets has now risen to a higher level and become airborne, Americans seem to be developing a certain tolerance for it. Maybe it is because travelers think they might get on television.

So far, Washington hasn't come up with any workable suggestions. It may be the administration considers hijacking one of those sectors reserved for private enterprise to deal with.

Does this mean hijacking is here to stay if there is some way it could be made to show a profit?

Considering the forthright way big business deals with things, one possible solution from the private sector is to expand Disney World. A small island, shaped like Cuba, could be built off the coast of Florida. Instead of all those hijacked airplanes landing in Havana, full of people with travel money, the hijacker could be tricked into landing at a duplicate place which would be more fun. It would be an easy switch, since there is no great problem making airports look alike.

Once landed, Spanish-speaking FBI agents could board the plane dressed whimsically as Cuban officials, arrest the confused hijacker in a jovial, courteous manner and not jeopardize his rights.

After this is done, an actor playing the part of Castro could be on hand to extend a cordial welcome to everyone and invite them all to take a fun-tour of Havanaland. Peter Ustinov, or someone not too terrifying in a beard, might be persuaded to play the part.

On the good chance that a lot of these hijackers are either Cuban agents or have a Tinkertoy mentality, television coverage would have to be discouraged. Fidel Castro watches it.

But the government will probably be the one to solve it, and in some boring, inefficient manner such as offering free one-way tickets to Cuba via Mexico City. That way, Washington would know anyone taking the hijack route was a Cuban agent for sure.

DRAINING BRITAIN

Three years ago Britain and France started implementing the plan for a tunnel under the English Channel, which apparently no one has wanted since it was first suggested in 1802. The unpopularity of European tourists may have been to blame. Of course, in 1802 it was probably that imminent French tourist, Napoleon, who was high on the unpopularity list.

But now the Brits want it even more than the French. This is because whimsical rumors have been going around that its construction will cause the French climate to seep up into London through the tubes. Certainly the wily French will not allow this to happen.

What is going to happen will boggle the imagination. England has been plugged up, so to speak, since the time of King Canute and through the centuries the only way for the English to get out of their weather, was to spend years building ships.

It was slow work to get out of England in those days but now French President François Mitterrand and British Prime Minister Margaret Thatcher have created a juggernaut. With the tunnel opened up, it will be like pulling the plug on a bathtub. The entire population of England and most of Scotland will be drained off onto the French Riviera within a matter of months, leaving nothing ambulatory south of the River Clyde.

In practical terms it sounds wonderful to go from London to Paris in less than four hours. So far no one has estimated the time from Paris to London, which may indicate no one has thought of going in that direction.

At this time the plan includes only traveling through the tunnel by train. This is very sensible, since it won't seem any different from the underground.

But it won't be until they build a road for cars and trucks that traffic will determine what the mean average speed is between London and Paris. Instead of bragging about it being less than four hours, it might be closer to less than four days.

Remarks will be made that swimming the channel is faster.

And, of course, one will quickly learn how to blow his horn in French.

GOOD GUYS GET THE BEEPS

For some reason I am no longer a threat to airport security. But there was a time when I could not get within 20 feet of a checkpoint without setting electrical systems into a frenzy of buzzers, beeps, and flashing lights that would shame a pinball machine.

WHY IS IT THAT ALARMS ARE SOUNDED WHEN INNOCENT PEOPLE LIKE ME GO THROUGH THE GATE?

Since I am at heart the antipode of a terrorist, I can only presume that these devices are consumed with some kind of bias against me. Why is it that alarms are sounded when innocent people like me go through the gate while all kinds of thugs walk on through without a single jingle?

When signals began to scream upon my approach, the usual procedure was for two female officials to close in and usher me to one side—away from innocent people. Then they would go over my entire person with a Geiger-like gadget that elicited hysterical ticking sounds out of every part of me.

One guard even asked, "Do you have any plates in your head?"

I answered in the negative, although one had been dropped on me recently.

The worst part was having to empty my pockets. One time I had to lay out a handful of diamonds. Of course they were *fake* diamonds from a theatrical performance, but within 20 minutes the entire concourse was filled with FBI agents.

Another embarrassing scene was taking out five bottle caps. They are not lethal weapons, but they do arouse intense suspicions as to why anyone would be carrying them.

I could see those ferretlike people mulling it over and sizing me up as a communist.

Lately my wife has been going through my pockets. Her digs have removed paper clips, a shoehorn from the Hilton, an airplane lapel pin with a free-spinning prop, a small screwdriver, and other odds and ends. Some of our friends think this is why I now go through security checks with comparative ease.

But I'm not so sure.

It's more likely that mechanical devices have stopped regarding me as an enemy. After all, computers do take on a life of their own.

BACK IN THE U.S.S.R.

IVAN, YOU'VE GOT TO LEARN TO STEER THESE THINGS
USSR
BONK

BUMPS IN THE ATLANTIC

Now that the public is aware that Soviet and US submarines, battleships, and aircraft carriers are constantly bumping into each other on maneuvers out in the middle of all that ocean, it may be time to think a little more about the world's sense of defense.

In the case of a Soviet submarine banging into the American aircraft carrier Kitty Hawk, or vice versa, the reassuring statement was made that if this had been a wartime situation, the submarine would never have gotten near the US battle group.

Everyone feel relieved? Of course, it's nice to be reminded now and then we are not in a wartime situation.

If the fleet at Pearl Harbor had been in a wartime situation back in December 1941, probably no Japanese bombers would have gotten inside the US defense perimeter either. Explanations like this do have their place.

It is just that the uninformed man in the street can hardly tell a "wartime situation" anymore. At least not without a score card. And it suggests, ever so slightly, that the military minds in the Pentagon can't tell the difference, either.

One thing does seem obvious. The Kitty Hawk, with all personnel, could have been blown higher than an orbiting space station, wartime or no wartime.

It has been reported that only one of the Navy's 14 aircraft carriers has any underwater detection sonar. Since it isn't necessary on 13 of the carriers, some confused civilian is going to wonder why it is so necessary on just one.

The US blames the Soviet submarine for the recent collision. It's nice to settle that point. Still, there is just that little nagging uncertainty. Ordinary citizens know there is something terribly stupid involved here. But being so unmilitary they don't know what it is.

ABOMINABLE SNOWMEN

Some strange areas of urgency are developing in the superpower race.

The Soviet Union is pushing hard to be ahead in the field of modern science. It is first to establish a space station and is ahead in man-time in space. The USSR is also believed to be ahead in preparing a manned flight to Mars.

But here's the latest area in which the Soviets have taken the lead: They are first to create an official society within their Ministry of Culture to find the abominable snowman. The abominable snowman, as most every tabloid reader knows, is also known throughout Asia as *yeti.* The Soviet news service Tass says there have been at least 100 sightings of this human-like monster in various out-of-the-way places, although the sightings have been made, apparently, by no one with any great reputation for sobriety.

What has official Washington been doing to challenge the USSR in this field? Zilch. Americans are taking second place in still another enterprise. The administration has piled up a $3 trillion deficit, spending money on heaven knows what. But not one cent has been allocated to finding an abominable snowman. Soon the Russians will not only be ahead in tanks, atomic bombs, and spacecraft, but abominable snowmen as well.

According to reports, this creature resembles prehistoric Neanderthal man. For some unexplained reason he has not progressed much since 50,000 BC, but he probably carries a big club to bash polar bears in order to survive. He must be terribly shy. For thousands of years he has made no meaningful contacts. People from outer space have allegedly done better.

If the Soviets do capture a cooperative *yeti* roaming around Siberia, he might well be eligible for Soviet citizenship with all the privileges that entails—a job, an apartment, and restricted traveling privileges. Chances are that he would not be permitted to visit relatives in Finland, or wherever.

There is always the possibility he might defect to the United States. This would even things up a bit. An abominable snowman isn't a space station, but it's something.

GLASNOST IN THE AIR

WE BELIEVE MATHIAS RUST MUST HAVE BEEN FLYING A STEALTH CESSNA

What are the full facts of the bizarre flight in 1987 of that German youth from Helsinki, through 400 miles of Soviet air defense systems and landing in Red Square, Moscow, next to the Kremlin? Some think this is just a fuller expression of *glasnost,* or the new openness of the Soviet borders. This isn't very likely. It was probably something else.

What we believe happened was that Mathias Rust, a young 19-year-old, must have been flying a United States Stealth Cessna 172B, with a top-secret engine capable of speeds up to 130 miles per hour and even higher if the pilot was wearing only shorts and a T-shirt. In addition, the plane may have been painted with the standard white paint formula which makes it almost invisible in the northern latitudes of Russia.

Although the Stealth Cessna can carry a bomb load of 23 hand grenades (which can be thrown out the window, or dropped through a hole in the floor) it was totally unarmed for this flight. Amazingly, it flew through 400 miles of antiballistic systems, an area impacted with 2,200 interceptor fighter planes, airborne warning planes, 10,000 radar stations, and more than 9,000 surface-to-air missiles—to say nothing of an extensive antiaircraft network.

Noticeably, there are no giggles coming out of the Pentagon. Quite possibly, the reason for this is that at least 50 Cessnas fly through the US air defense system every week without much interference, landing anyplace in Florida, Georgia, Texas, and other southwest areas to unload tons of cocaine.

Europeans know this. The flight of Mathias Rust notwithstanding, they remember the commercial airliner shot down off the Siberian coast with all lives lost. They know which of the superpowers *really* has control of its extensive borders.

The only possible reason a Cessna didn't land on Pennsylvania Avenue in front of the White House is that Nancy Reagan said "no" to drugs. But if one does land there one can be sure there will be months of congressional investigation on TV. It should be a great show.

HOT HANDS, COLD FEET

As the cold war between the United States and the Soviet Union comes closer to ending, why do my feet keep getting colder?

I know that people living in *glasnost* houses shouldn't throw stones, but there is something slightly like the pitch of a used-car-salesman in Gorbachev's assurance that European stability is just a matter of getting rid of all the intermediate- and short-range missiles. Gorbachev doesn't even look like Khrushchev or Brezhnev. He looks like someone's kindly, European uncle. Reagan looks like somebody's uncle too, but it's Uncle Sam everyone thinks of.

Once all the dirty old nukes are gone, it leaves the Soviets with a nice clean superiority in conventional weapons—especially tanks—and it is still less than 500 kilometers from West Germany to the English channel. Gorbachev, with a smile, agrees to talk about conventional weapons, but only after all the nukes are gone. Meanwhile Europe might feel something like Finland.

In the midst of all this, the friendly Russians have been sending spies into the American Embassy, through the front door, by the simple device of overcoming American Marines with friendly Russian girls, who no doubt were dressed in the new *glasnost* styles. Apparently it didn't take very long to change the Marine motto to Simper Fidelis.

Even the new American Embassy, which was built by the friendly Russians, was planted so full of bugs the KGB can hear the moths eating the woolen blankets.

Reducing nuclear arms can be desirable if other things are equal. It would be nice if the Soviet Union could reduce its military hold on Eastern Europe in the spirit of *glasnost*. Eventual danger lurks more in the political than the nuclear differences.

Russia still holds many advantages. Not least among them is that any time it wants to rearrange any agreement, it takes only the blink of an eye in Moscow. The US must not only go through its democratic process at home but involve itself in lengthy negotiations with its European allies.

Up until now the nuclear capability of the US has been considered a sort of umbrella for Western Europe. Just as Western Europe is getting adjusted to the umbrella idea, along comes Uncle Mikhail playing his balalaika and singing, "It ain't goin' to rain no more . . . ."

'COMRADE, ONE OF OUR FREIGHT TRAINS IS MISSING'

Incidental intelligence, unrelated to anything, turns up now and then in the American press the way cats turn up in the backyard, looking like a cat you had 10 years ago.

According to a news item I stumbled across, the Soviet Union lost a freight train. Losing a 28-car freight train seems a little strange, even for the Soviet Union, so I tried to find out if anything like this ever happened in the United States.

The best I could come up with is that US trucking companies lose a truck now and then. These are hijacked, and are filled with fabulous objects such as computers or TV sets. The Russian train was full of crushed rock.

Anyway, the news item didn't imply that someone stole it. Apparently the entire 28-car freight train just got lost.

The train left a Ukrainian crushed-rock factory and never got to where it was going. Two years later, it was still missing. It is reasonable to suppose the train stayed on the tracks and had to go wherever the tracks went, so it seems that if searchers just kept on following the tracks they would find the train. Such was not the case, evidently, because it never turned up.

Soviet officials have now discontinued the search, because documents on freight deliveries are kept only for one year and then destroyed. If the documents no longer exist, then it stands to reason the train doesn't, either. I have done some superficial research just recently to be sure the case was finished and also to find out if any more trains had disappeared. As far as I could discover, no more trains were lost, but they did lose one tank.

The lost-tank mystery was finally solved, however. They found that someone had dismantled it and sold it for spare parts.

Meanwhile, I wonder about the lost 28-car freight train and all that crushed rock. I like to think that some enterprising Muscovite put the crushed rock into packages and sold them for souvenirs. There must be a lot of lonely misplaced Ukrainians around who would yearn for a bit of Ukrainian crushed rock to remind them of home.

Oddly enough, I find no mention of any lost engineers.

MOON OVER MOSCOW

It has been reported on good authority that the Soviet Union is already making plans to colonize the moon and Mars before the end of the century. This burst of good news will give fresh hope to all those who have been trying to get out of Russia.

All through history the Russians have been prevented from reaching out to gain access to a better climate. It now seems they are going to make it.

THAT THERE IS NO FREE, BREATHABLE AIR ON THE MOON PRESENTS NO SERIOUS DETERRENT TO SOVIET CITIZENS

The fact that there is no free, breathable air on either the moon or Mars presents no serious deterrent to Soviet citizens, since as they point out, everything is relative. Many expect it to be easier to breathe on the moon than in Moscow. Lack of water presents no serious hazard, either. It means no more snow. And the weekly Saturday night bath can be taken just as well in a tub of vodka.

No doubt some thought has been given to making Mars or the moon the new Siberia, providing an even more secure place to send political dissenters. While the new locations would be comparatively escape proof, the Kremlin might hesitate to give prisoners a better place to live than Muscovy factory workers.

Basically, it is weather that sends a nation's people out beyond their borders, seeking new frontiers. Englishmen spread themselves over the entire world just to get away from the English winter and find someplace with sunshine. Russia had a horrible climate, too, but Russians didn't go anywhere because it is too difficult to get a passport out of the country.

How long it will take the Soviet Union to put a substantial population on the moon has not been disclosed, but it will behoove the United States to keep its space program in high gear. Once Lunar Moscow is established, complete with factories, stolen computer parts, and a five-year program, Congress will find itself involved in a new debate over Soviet relations.

But in the end, the US will have to have some way to ship wheat up there.

SAVE VENUS

There is an ominous development going on which the general media seem unaware of. Just at the time when the Soviet Union is supplying arms for revolution to Central America through Cuba, news comes that the Soviets are landing spaceships on Venus in relatively large numbers.

Back in December of 1978, two Russian spacecraft landed there within a short time of each other. Now there are two more. According to the official Soviet Tass news agency they are unmanned.

There may be no need for alarm in all this, but it behooves the United States to look at this situation calmly and objectively. What, for instance, does Venus have in the way of strategic position? At best it is a vapor-shrouded planet with a bad, gassy climate and would be a thoroughly unpleasant outpost, even for Russians, who are used to these conditions.

However, it has been well pointed out that this planet is close to the sun, which is a main source of heat and light, not only for the US but the entire free world. This heat and light source would be, for many, the only feasible alternate to the Russian gas line from Siberia.

All this is happening at the very moment nuclear power plants all over the US are blowing out valves and tubes and leaking some kind of tainted hydrogen all over the place. If anything points to the need of continued solar energy, this does.

The current administration, regardless of its eagerness to balance the budget, is going to have to adopt some sort of foreign policy to deal with this new Soviet maneuvering. It is hoped that this could be done without too many congressional hearings and too much panic in the press. One possible response would be for the free world jointly to approach Venus in a friendly and cooperative manner. Certainly we should make the average Venusian see that an association with the free and democratic US is more beneficial and attractive to him than the dour, one-party mentality of Russia.

One word of caution: it may turn out that if there is any sensible life on Venus, it may be even more dour and depressed than that in Moscow. The creatures may have lived on hot asphalt for so long (being close to the sun) that Siberian tundra sounds like the Garden of Eden.

I
LOVE
EUЯOPE

GRIN-AND-BEAR POLICY

Once in a while we get to chuckling uncontrollably at Soviet foreign policy.

Soviet foreign policy is funny in a different way from Washington foreign policy. The Moscow brand has a ballet quality: a clever magician producing a chicken from his sleeve and finding it has laid an egg.

What would international news be without it? What would a presidential election in the US be without a candidate who stood up to communism? If only Gilbert and Sullivan were alive.

The Soviet Union is currently playing a conciliatory overture to its archenemy, China. This isn't because the Russians have started trusting the Chinese but because the Chinese are sending nasty remarks in their fortune cookies to the US, owing to a hangup over Taiwan.

But the music Brezhnev is composing for China is a concert played with mittens on. What little harmony there might be is surely lost in the explosions from Afghanistan, which, like China, shares a border with the USSR. The music sent out may be a lullaby, but what China will hear is a sort of 1812 Overture.

At the same time Russia is orchestrating policy toward China in the East, it is also playing a persuasive solo on the flute toward the West, promising not to deploy any more missiles, aimed at Europe, in exchange for a zero deployment from NATO. Since Brezhnev already has 300 medium-range missiles in position, the NATO ministers have rejected this. But it has a sweet-toned, pied-piper effect on the portions of the population in Europe which want no missiles deployed in their own country.

What is funny in this case is not the bear dressing up in dove's clothing but its actually presenting itself as Europe's protector. From big bully to big brother. A sort of super, Moscow-based NATO.

It gives us the picture of a bear, gently holding a salmon in its mouth, promising never to bite down.

HEROES AND TURKEYS

THE GREAT ADVANTAGES OF LIVING IN THE SOVIET UNION ARE APPARENT TO EVERYONE EXCEPT SOVIET HEROES

Heroes are not what they used to be. Everyone knows that.

Everyone except Moscow. In Moscow, the decline in heroes has evidently become a national disgrace.

According to a Reuters account, Pravda has been urged to point out that heroes in the Soviet Union are becoming oblivious to their communist convictions. Pravda further points out that from now on Soviet heroes should display more fidelity to their social and patriotic duty. Furthermore, they should embody "a firm ideological stance, political vigilance, and a reliable Marxist-Leninist arsenal," and thus show the evident advantages of Soviet life.

There's the whole trouble with heroes: They don't know when they are well off.

What can be done in a situation like this? The great advantages of living in the Soviet Union are apparent to everyone except Soviet heroes. Housewives, workers, artists, generals, are all happy with their lot, their government would have us believe—so why are Soviet heroes so stupid?

Evidently there is a corrupting influence somewhere that needs correcting. The entire fiction-loving public of the world can sympathize with whoever is in charge of Soviet heroes these days, because if he can't come up with a James Bond, a Superman, or even a Wonder Woman, what has he got? Karl Marx on a motorcycle?

Karl Marx may have had a "firm ideological stance" and "political vigilance," but he would be zilch in the love scenes even if he could get on and off a horse, or wear swim trunks.

Lenin would be just as bad. A flying Lenin, fighting for truth and justice and the Soviet way, complete with red cape and a big, capital "L" on his chest, would be a complete turkey. If Russia has turkeys.

Then there is always another problem. As soon as a satisfactory hero emerges, such as a tennis player, ballet dancer, or airplane pilot, he or she flees the Soviet Union sooner or later, political vigilance notwithstanding.

Moscow does have a problem with heroes: They tend to turn into ideological villains.

GASSING GAME

The Soviet Union has found great quantities of natural gas up in Siberia, and the idea of letting it seep down into Europe is the most original plot since the witch gave a bad apple to Snow White.

One might wonder if the Soviets have invented a more civilized version of gas warfare. Instead of breathing it, you burn it in your furnace. Instead of having it ooze all around you like California smog, you can buy it cheap in easy monthly payments. The fact that the Russians are selling it to Europe in a pipe gives Secretary of State Haig as much concern, if not more, than the mycotoxins he says they are fumigating Afghanistan with.

Just at the time when Russia is making warm friends with gas, President Reagan is losing them with hot air. Just at the time when the United States would like Europe to join in a common front of sanctions against the USSR over Poland, France and the rest of Europe are becoming sheep in sheep's clothing. After all, it's only those offensively vociferous Poles who are going to suffer.

It is probably a case of Europe being so close to the Russian bear that it feels only the warmth of the furry hug. The US is far enough away to see the teeth.

How much effect pointing the gas line at France has had in the recent, rapid socialization of that country is a long-shot speculation. But it is enough to say that, much to the dismay of Western countries, France is once again meeting its problems the opposite of everybody else. Just when the free world is trying to fight the recession by getting government off the backs of the people, France is going piggyback in a big way. In fact Europe is getting so divided no one knows how to color a map anymore.

For Americans, the only thing harder to figure out than a mule on Sunday is a Frenchman. The American tends to think everyone should be like he is and want to breathe free enterprise air. The Frenchman will breathe anything so long as it's French.

But probably all this Siberian gas leaking into French homes won't have any lasting effect on the French. Nothing ever does. And the average Frenchman can't look at the average Russian very long without noticing he's not French. And then he will wake up from the pipedream.

WORD PLAY

NO SPEKA DA ENGLISH

HE BIT HIS SANDWICH AS IF IT WERE MY NECK . . . "EVERYONE SPEAKS SOME KIND OF ENGLISH. IT'S REVOLTING!"

At an afternoon lawn party I found myself sitting next to a bearded fellow who was mumbling. Thinking he was saying something to me, I leaned in his direction and said, "I beg your pardon?"

He leaned in my direction and said something like, "Lernas la lingvo Esperanto?" I gave him a blank look.

"Have you learned how to speak Esperanto?" he snapped. "It's the internacia lingvo! Por la tuto mondo!"

"I have a hard enough time learning to speak good English," I said in an effort to lighten the conversation. He bit his sandwich as if it were my neck. "I never find anyone who speaks it." He chewed scornfully. "Everyone speaks some kind of English. It's revolting!"

I tried to think of something helpful. "You speak a lot of languages?" I asked.

"A few," he actually smiled. "Besides English and Esperanto, I speak Ngulu, Edo, and Urdu."

This effectively stopped the conversation. I not only didn't speak any of the languages he mentioned, I wasn't sure who did. "Ngulu?" I finally whispered.

"Yes!" he exploded. "I had to learn Ngulu because no one in Mozambique spoke Esperanto. Stupidly they speak English, which is five times harder to learn."

I eventually learned that Esperanto was invented in 1887 by Dr. L. L. Zamenhof. Its use is gradually increasing, my friend thought, but not nearly as fast as English.

Perhaps the problem with Esperanto is that it will always be a second language. No one speaks only that. Yet the number of people who speak English as a second language is immense. I haven't seen my bearded friend since, but I presume he is still hoping Esperanto will be the "Lingvo por la tuto mondo."

A CHOWDER OF CATS, A KNOT OF TOADS . . .

Recently I had a conversation while sitting on the bench down at the bus stop with an old codger who was eating an ice cream cone.

He said, "Every day in my backyard we have a murder of crows."

"Murder of crows?" I queried, wishing the ice cream wouldn't drip on the front of his new sport shirt. "What kind of murder is that?"

"Murder," he said. "Back home that means a whole bunch of crows."

I can't say much for the rest of the conversation, which was mostly about how the hair was coming out of his cat. But his comments reminded me of a time I went to a friend's house for dinner. While the guests waited to be served, the young six-year-old daughter came in and said, "Hello. Tonight we have a chowder of cats."

The faces of all the guests turned a shade whiter than the tablecloth. Then I recalled something out of the mishmash of what I waggishly call a memory.

"I think what she means," I said, with an important resonance creeping into my voice, "is that she has a *clowder* of cats—or a clutter. It means *a bunch of*—like a gaggle of geese."

Later in the evening it was a relief to find a box of five small kittens in the garage, although by this time they were calling them a "kindle."

Driving home, one of the men in the car said, "I never heard the word clowder, but," he added proudly, "I've heard of a pod of whales. Pod, that's a real word."

His wife added her bit. "Down on the farm we used to say we had a clutch of chicks. That's a real word, too. It's in the dictionary."

She was right, of course. But I know there are a lot of unlisted plural words, more uncommon than flock (sheep), drove (cattle), covey (quail), or yoke (oxen), because my uncle used to refer to a knot of toads.

But a murder of crows?

Maybe he's right. Though some of these old geezers like to pull one's leg a bit.

I AIN'T A PRUDE, BUT . . .

By and large, I don't consider myself a prude. A prune, maybe, according to a few critical but unenlightened readers. But a prude? No. Except in a few minor cases where being a prude is the intelligent thing to be.

Where I am put to the test, however, is in listening to the English used on television, filling the already badly educated minds of our children. I readily agree English is a living, growing language, but that doesn't excuse the wanton and senseless destruction of it by commentators with million-dollar contracts. If they can't speak good English, why pay them so much?

A lot of them avoid the word "good" because a lot of morons on TV use "good" incorrectly. Therefore they all use the word "well" incorrectly to prove they have background. As one highly paid commentator said recently, "The dress looks well on Nancy." Oh, really? To me that conveys a picture of a dress full of eyes, peering in every direction. The dress looked *good* on Nancy. With annoying consistency commentators say things similar to, "It is difficult to deal with those kind of governments." Why can't they deserve their salary by saying, ". . . that kind of government"?

Oh, yes, I did go up the wall when an actress—one million dollars a picture—was asked where she got her expensive diamond necklace. "I get all my jewl-ery abroad," she said. I say if she doesn't know how to say jewelry, it ought to be snatched off her, then and there.

The word "hopefully" has gone beyond all hope. As one college football player said: "They won't win the game tomorrow, hopefully." Just once, can't some student, professor, senator, president, or man-in-the-street say, "I hope they won't win the game tomorrow"?

But, as I say, I am not a prude and English is a living language, so I can put up with questionable English when the wisdom involved outweighs the sensitivity for grammar. "If it ain't broke, don't fix it."

Then just when the day is going along pleasantly a theater critic asks a newly risen star when he will start his next picture. "Like November," is the answer.

We'll have to let it go at that.

I AIN'T A PRUDE, PART 2

Since there was such a large response to the "I ain't a prude" column, dealing with the English spoken on television, it seems only fair to do one more and include some of the pet peeves from readers. And one more will be the absolute end, even though it's like trying to describe what's wrong with the government on a post card.

One reader complains that Barbara Walters, when talking about art, always says "pitcher." On the other hand, Barbara Walters gets a lot of things right, so perhaps we shouldn't complain.

Several readers groan when TV personalities try to show their respect for proper speech by saying, "He will be with you and I." It is especially groanworthy when such mistakes are made by members of Congress who have just had a raise in salary. (They would probably say they got it "irregardless" of their objections.)

Most complaints come from readers about the ads done by prominent actors, using words like "diper," "Febuary," "realator," and phrases such as "most unique." There is a special complaint from my wife that commentators too often use the word "nucular" when talking about the bomb.

Speaking of bombs, it seems the biggest grammatical bombs are dropped by sportscasters: "It was him who made the score . . . " is commonplace. It seems to be a rule that anyone interested in sports is not allowed to use good English.

No less a lexicological deity than William Safire supports the correctness of "It is me," so one has to accept it. In his convoluted way he defends it as established idiom. What it boils down to is that if poor English is used persistently enough, it makes correct English seem pompous and thus to be avoided, which proves one can't fight city hall. And one can't fight city streets, either.

I think we should continue to insist on high standards of speech, even in a world where all standards seem to be pushed aside. At the same time we can be grateful that English, even when misspoken, can be understood, as in the case of the foreigner explaining to his friend why he had no children by saying his wife was "inconceivable."

His meaning was clear at least on the second time around.

FROM ONE GEEZER TO ANOTHER

Recently this column had a piece on the economics of social security and how this looming crisis affected the retired "old geezers" on the bench outside of the Arcade Quick Lunch. When we used the term "geezer" we unwittingly stepped into the line of fire from the shuffleboard court.

Since we count ourself as being a member of the old geezers of America, we were surprised at the stormy objection to such a lovable term. We are now in more hot water than a backyard Jacuzzi.

Geezer, as dictionaries define it, is either a "person in disguise" or "an eccentric."

These terms may not fit everybody in the golden, or copper-pyrite, years, but they get a laugh over at the Mobile Home Park. The problem is, the whole category of retired persons, if it exists at all, is a stereotype. There is no typical retired person in spite of all the fatuous articles written by young authorities.

It has been our experience to find many—what shall we say?—"senior citizens" fit both definitions of geezer at least one day out of the week. There are some who work part time, or all the time, and some who do not. Some simply have a lot of fun doing things they never had time to do before. And, there are some, alas, who are very stoic and grim about what has been allotted to them by what we waggishly call society.

One "senior citizen," who had been a manager in an accounting firm, is now a "bag man" in a supermarket three days a week. He needs the money, naturally. Expenses go up, while his income is fixed.

He fits both definitions of geezer. His orange slacks and flamingo shirt are a kind of disguise from his former gray-suit-and-tie uniform. His floppy hat, pinned full of fishing lures, makes him a bit eccentric. Except on weekends, when he is actually catching fish.

In our days as cartoonist we had our nose punched once in a while. Now we admire what is left of it and would like to keep it intact. So we hereby make a sweeping apology to all the nongeezers of America.

We know there are a lot of whatchamacallums out there who do not play checkers and shuffleboard, pick up shells, sit on benches (provided by banks, drugstores, and restaurants), or go to church in shorts. Just the same, a better term than geezer has not yet occurred to us.

But we're working on it.

SIR, I'M FORMING AN OLD GEEZER'S CLUB...
GREAT! WHAT'S AN OLD GEEZER?

IT'S AN ENIGMA

It all started one day while I was in a holding pattern somewhere between New York and Boston. Out of frustration and boredom due to the monotonous delay, I asked the fellow next to me where he was from.

MY FRIEND NEXT TO ME WHISPERED, "ASK HER IF SHE'S EVER HEARD OF A PLACE IN TEXAS NAMED CUT AND SHOOT."

"Enigma," he said.

"I'm sorry," I said. "I didn't mean to pry."

"Enigma," he replied. "That's 20 miles from Mystic."

It turned out that indeed he lived in Georgia near a town called Enigma. The conversation could have happily stopped there, but he offered additional information that he had a relative living in Deaf Smith, Texas. He said when his relative told people where he was from, they always said, "What?"

The lady sitting across the aisle, who overheard our conversation, apparently had some connection with the United Nations. She forced herself into the dialogue by saying that people might well not know places in the United States but that there was no excuse for not knowing about independent countries of the world.

"I find hardly anyone has ever heard of Kiribati," she said.

This didn't surprise me. I had never heard of Kiribati myself. For all I knew, it was something found in a dish of Japanese sashimi, and I couldn't see the connection with Deaf Smith, Texas.

"People simply don't know the names of the places of the world they live in," she continued. "For instance, Lesotho . . . ."

Well, I happened to know where Lesotho was, but she delightedly told me it was a kingdom ruled by King Moshoeshoe. The name came across the aisle as "More Shoe Shoe," so the man next to me laughed in appreciation. It made the lady angry and more aggressive.

"Now take the Republic of Vanuatu . . . ."

"Vanuatu?" I said. "Vanuatu?"

"We are cleared out of our holding pattern," the captain said over the speaker system.

My friend next to me whispered, "Ask her if she's ever heard of a place in Texas named Cut and Shoot."

But I had had enough. I pushed my seat back, hoping for a nap, grateful that my average traveling involved only places with sensible names, like Sarasota, Atlanta, New York, and Boston.

SWEET INSINCERITY

Recently I kept track of the number of times in one day that someone told me to "Have a good day." Up until 2 p.m. it was 18 times, which just about reaches the level of tolerance for any law-abiding citizen. I lost track after someone said, "Have a *nice* day," instead of "Have a good day." The word "nice" has a pink-ribbon sound that sets my teeth on edge.

I'm not sure when the omniscient and long-winded version of "Good day" got started, but I have noticed it over the last few years with ever-mounting aversion and a continuing urge to stick my finger in the speaker's eye. I suppose it is better than people hoping you have a lousy day, or suggesting you stick your head in a pickle crock.

The trouble is, there is something about the way "Have a good day" is said which indicates no real concern whether you have a good day or not. Actors say, "Go break a leg," but they don't mean that, either. Maybe sweet insincerity is just more tolerable than candor.

As a sample of how meaningless this pronouncement has become, once I was discussing with the Internal Revenue Service a mistake that was to cost me $3,000, and the agent rang off with "You have a good day, now!" In like manner I was wished a good day by a lady after she backed into my car at a parking lot, which cost me $185.57. I suppose the day could have been worse, but it could have been better without her insipid command.

No doubt this all stems from an effort to be polite in a world where politeness is vanishing faster than service at a gas station. (Remember back when they used to be called service stations?) But the human psyche can stand only so much platitude before the social graces break down and someone gets a pie in the face.

One day our standard greeting may change to something else. Some save-the-language group organized out of desperation will come up with a new trend like: "Have a fair-to-middling day."

It would certainly seem more in keeping with the political outlook of the times.

IT'S ALL IN THE PAST

IMAGINE !!
100,000 YEARS
AGO THEY WERE
DRINKING COKE..

THE SMELL OF YOUTH

There is a place near where I live in Florida called Warm Mineral Springs, which is being considered as a National Historic Landmark. This comes as a surprise to many old-time residents, because not too many years ago it was considered a mudhole.

Now it is thought to be landmark material for a number of reasons.

For one thing, the waters are supposed to be healthy even though they don't smell that way—the "mineral" content being mostly sulfur. Another thing, even though the springs have been prettied up a bit, some serious-looking scholars of the area believe this to be the Fountain of Youth discovered by Ponce de León. Whether Ponce got any younger as a result of dipping into this place is doubtful. In fact, some maintain there is a distinct possibility that it made him older, since the waters have never been described as delicious.

Perhaps the main reason the springs have National Landmark validity is that down in the 45-foot depths are fossils and artifacts of archaeological significance which have recently been discovered.

Divers have found a 100,000-year-old mammoth down there which may be some evidence the mammoths and other creatures of the Pleistocene age found the waters therapeutic. Either that, or one good swig finished them off.

Along with the ancient bones an assortment of Coca-Cola and Dr. Pepper bottles have been found. I believe there was also a bedspring, circa 1934.

Once Warm Mineral Springs has been approved by the secretary of the interior of the United States, it will rate right along with the Statue of Liberty and Independence Hall—even the White House—as a National Historic Landmark. At the present time Warm Mineral Springs doesn't seem in a class to offer tourist competition with the White House, unless they find it really is the Fountain of Youth.

I hope that won't be the case. Such a discovery might sink Florida.

THE OLD GIZA

One of the hairiest problems to deal with in today's world is whether or not to put the beard back on the Sphinx.

At one time, they say the Sphinx had a very impressive beard, but most of it has been cracked off by wind and sand over 4,500 years.

Whatever was left, the British took back to London and put in the British Museum. Just why it is more important to have the Sphinx's beard in a museum rather than on the Sphinx's chin is not easy to understand. Presumably the British believe there is some archaeological value in not only seeing a Sphinx without a beard, but also a beard without a Sphinx.

At any rate, it was undoubtedly too inconvenient to move the whole Sphinx to London. Half the museum would have to be torn down to get the Sphinx inside, and even then it might not go with the frieze from the Parthenon.

What remains of the Sphinx sits in its original place, without the beard. Many think being beardless makes him look younger. It may be true, give or take 1,300 years, but even without a beard he is a long way from John Travolta.

But being handsome isn't everything. A young, handsome face really doesn't make it, Sphinxwise. The deep wisdom of the ages requires the whiskered look.

If the answer hung on these points alone, the issue might be debated for centuries. But there is another problem, which has to do with the neck. Beards, it seems, are a protection to necks.

Human necks suffer only wrinkles and ring around the collar.

However, a beardless Sphinx gets thinner and thinner around the neck as years go by, until it cracks up and the head rolls off.

A plastic beard has been suggested, which is certainly indicative of the times. It predicts a rather awesome trend. Replacing worn parts with plastic would eventually result in an all-plastic Sphinx. If this is to be the result, it might be better to do it all at once and get it over with. Of course, a plastic Sphinx would probably offend historic purists.

It is a pity these ancient monuments aren't all they are cracked up to be.

MILKMEN OF YESTERYEAR

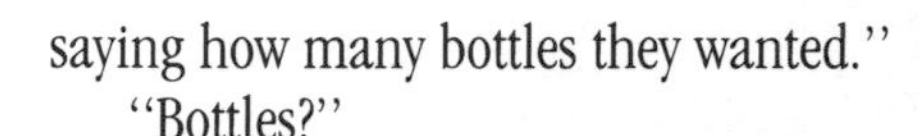

Several days ago I fell into a generation gap. I try not to fall into them more than once a week, but sometimes I run over.

I was talking to a 10-year-old friend about my father. In the conversation I said, "His best friend was a milkman."

"A what?" said the youngster.

"A milkman," I answered matter-of-factly.

"What was he? Made out of milk?"

This kid seemed a bit stupid. "No," I said flatly. "He *delivered* milk. Also butter and eggs. Like the iceman delivered ice!"

The kid's eyes glazed over. "People carried milk and eggs and ice around? For what?"

Evidently this is what happens. Whole pieces of social planking drop out of the structure of history. I can remember milkmen clearly. I can even remember they were the last to give up horses for delivery, because going along a street the horse remembered which house to stop at better than the milkman did.

I could see the youngster really didn't know what I was talking about, so I explained. "People left a note at the door saying how many bottles they wanted."

"Bottles?"

"Yes, bottles. Milk came in bottles. The milkman would pick up the empties, put them in the rack he carried, and leave full ones. Then the people would bring them in and take the cream off . . . ."

"Cream? There was a bottle of cream stacked on top of the bottle of milk?"

"No," I said patiently. "The cream was *in* the milk. The top half of the bottle . . . ."

I could see this was slightly confusing information, so I didn't bother to introduce ragmen to the conversation. Neither did I mention scissor-grinders, who came around fairly often to sharpen our kitchen knives. But I couldn't let him off too easily.

"Later on in the day," I said, to give him something to think about, "the waffleman came by. I could get a crisp, freshly cooked waffle, covered with powdered sugar, for a penny."

When I left, the kid was talking to a friend and pointing in my direction—probably telling him I was from another planet.

And I guess I was.

THE TERRIFIC PALEOLITHIC

There is an exhibit in New York at the American Museum of Natural History concerning the Upper Paleolithic Age. Don't be misled by the big word. To the average paleontologist this is modern history, like World War I.

The people of upper paleolithic times, which were more or less between 15,000 and 35,000 years ago, are essentially no different from the Europeans of today.

This is the time when Cro-Magnon man, or Homo sapiens, came upon the scene. That's us.

This modern-looking, Cro-Magnon man replaced the Neanderthals who ruled the European continent for some 60,000 years, give or take a year. When the handsome, inventive, enterprising Cro-Magnons replaced the Neanderthals, it zipped our civilization along at an accelerated rate.

So, naturally, the Cro-Magnons are considered the good guys and the Neanderthals the bad guys in the paleolithic scenario.

Well, everyone has heard of the bad-guy Neanderthals. They were physical giants and could lift about 1,000 pounds of woolly mammoth if they had to, but they were all hair and probably had bad breath.

They were also ugly specimens with awful sloping foreheads, heavy brows, protruding teeth, and massive jaws. In short, they had the same profile as an anvil.

As far as looks were concerned, one could say they came out a poor second to the prehistoric wart hog.

Neanderthals started about 100,000 years ago. They were the first toolmakers, and they did walk upright on their hind legs, but that's about as far as they got.

When the Cro-Magnons came along, they weren't as massive but they had the smarts. They could do everything better. Scientists believe that when the Cro-Magnons took over the scene, the Neanderthals entirely disappeared from the earth.

Maybe they didn't entirely disappear. It seems to me that I keep running into a few of them every so often in a Wal-Mart department store. And I'm sure there are a number of them on TV videos.

If they appear again today in the world of complete nondiscrimination, they won't disappear; they will be nurtured. If a hairy tribe of them loped into the lobby of the Ritz-Carlton they would not only be tolerated, but with modern concepts of "neutral vision" which makes everything of equal value, they might even come to be in charge again.

It's an odd paradox. Intelligent discrimination 15,000 years ago accelerated achievement into our modern high level of civilization.

Homo sapiens!

May we always have the practical sense to live up to our name.

It is high time that Lightly readers were made aware of the "Mokele-Mbembe" before it is too late.

According to Jim Culberson, a graduate in marine biology from Florida Institute of Technology who has been in Africa researching these things, Mokele-Mbembe is a 40-foot species of dinosaur which has been seen roaming the Congo.

HE HAS SEEN PICTURES . . . TAKEN OF FRESH FOOTPRINTS 'ABOUT AS LARGE AS A FRYING PAN'

Dinosaurs were supposed to have disappeared with a bang in the Cretaceous Period and haven't been seen for about 350 million years, so if there are a few living in Africa at the present time it is going to make a better movie than King Kong.

A 40-foot dinosaur may not seem like much, since dinosaurs reached a length of 100 feet. But when one considers the wear and tear of surviving 350 million years on short rations, 40 feet is quite impressive. Anyway, it is bigger than an elephant. And if they were much bigger, everyone would see one.

Culberson has been searching certain areas where the natives claim to have encountered the Mokele-Mbembe and are none the worse for it. He has seen pictures, he says, taken of fresh footprints and he states that "the tracks are about as large as a frying pan with three toes out front."

The habitat of these dinosaurs is deep in a 60,000-mile area known as the Likouala Swamp where it must be difficult to find things, even if they are 40 feet long. Culberson is planning on going back for another search in spite of the skeptical remarks from other scientists.

"The scientific community thinks we are nuts," Culberson says. ". . . but what you have to understand is that most of the scientists who consider us fringe flakes are armchair scientists. They have not been in there." "In there" presumably meaning in that Likouala Swamp—and anyone spending much time in the Likouala Swamp could change his mind about a lot of things.

Culberson is raising some money and hopes he will find Mokele-Mbembe on his next trip. One can't rule it out as impossible. There is a huge, prehistoric monster up at Loch Ness, Scotland, so why couldn't there be some related monsters hiding out in the darker reaches of the Congo?

INTO THE END ZONE

FRED THE SOFA

Once in a while, when my wife and her next-door friend go on a shopping spree, I reward myself by eating at a tablecloth restaurant.

On this particular day I was seated at a single table just behind a table with two ladies in a talkative mood. One lady was rather large, with blue hair; the other, somewhat narrower, had crisply curled brownish hair. She was the listener. Big Blue was the talker.

They lifted glasses frequently, toyed with salads, and dabbed with napkins while I sat waiting for my Trout Almondine. Big Blue was talking: "You know how some people grow to look like their pets? Well, my husband, Fred, has gotten to look like a sofa."

I am not usually an eavesdropper, but in this case I thought it might be my duty as a member of the fraternal order of husbands to record mentally what was being said about the unsuspecting Fred.

Big Blue continued: "You can shake your head all you want, Emma, but two nights ago I said good night to just the sofa. Fred wasn't even in the house and I didn't notice the difference. So, you see!"

Brown Hair pretended to laugh and said, "Now, now, now, you know perfectly well that after your party last week the couch got covered with gravy stains. So that's one way you can tell which is which."

"Fred is also covered with gravy stains."

My salad came and that threw my concentration off for several sentences. When I tuned in again, Big Blue was still going on:

"It's football, football, football. He sits on one end of the sofa for three or four hours at a stretch. He absorbs the sofa. He shouts at stupid players. He even gets to talking gibberish and mumbles names like 'Bucs,' 'Noles,' and 'Skins.'

By the time I left, Fred had been pretty well reduced to the form, design, and color of a sofa cushion. Unlike Fred, I hardly ever look at a football game, so I considered my wife pretty fortunate she didn't have to live with a sofa cushion.

When I finally got home, friend wife was back from shopping and wanted to know my afternoon plans.

"The US Open tennis matches are on," I said, heading for the television. "I've already missed the first 10 minutes."

I didn't know why she gave me the look she did. Maybe it was the gravy stain on my shirt.

GRIDIRONY

STUDIES OF UNITED STATES MARITAL HABITS TEND TO PROVE THAT MORE WIVES LEAVE HOME DURING FOOTBALL SEASON THAN ANY OTHER TIME

Football players have gone on strike. While this is not expected to raise unemployment over 10 percent, it does raise a few eyebrows. NFL football players not only want to call the signals down on the field, they would also like to call the signals up in the office.

In this regard, it is unfortunate that pictures of American football players present a huge, gargantuan body with a very small head. This is simply not the management image.

Maybe the football players just need to change their uniform from dirty jersey to silk tie, pin-stripe suit, and cleated oxfords.

In a poll regarding the strike and thus the absence of Sunday football on television, one-third of the people questioned said, "Who cares?" Obviously this poll didn't include women. Otherwise the "Who cares?" attitude would have been well over 50 percent. Studies of United States marital habits tend to prove that more wives leave home during football season than any other time—and that the husbands didn't even know it until after the playoffs.

Many social reformers aver that the end of football would bring new vitality to marriage, a resurgence of lawn care covering 12 million acres, and the repair of leaks in 256,000 kitchen faucets conserving an estimated 100 million gallons of water.

One fact seems clear. The players didn't think up the strike. Lawyers thought up the strike. Just the heady aroma of $1.6 billion being passed around out on the football field is enough to bring lawyers in their Mercedeses from every state in the Union. Countless alleged whiplash victims are left helpless in anterooms, waiting in vain for the usual million-dollar settlement.

Big rewards for athletes are not new. In early Roman days the gladiators (forerunners of NFL veterans) got big rewards. Of course, the biggest reward of all was not to be eaten by a lion. Coliseum owners of today don't have this convincing advantage. Today lions are in short supply. Anyway, a game between the Los Angeles Raiders and 11 lions would probably end in a tie.

Cleats and Tutus: Super Performances

It may sound strange, but I didn't see Super Bowl XIX.

It isn't that I don't like the game of football. I used to play a game of the same name in my school days, although it was somewhat different. I presume that was because it wasn't on television.

Pro football and college football are closely related now. I don't always understand the difference.

We had a coach, but he also coached all the other sports the school had, and I'm sure we never had a choreographer. We practiced only basic football. None of the players ever had an agent. Now that agents have come into the game, I presume it is only a matter of time before football players join Equity. Or maybe they already belong to Equity. I'm not always the first to know something.

When I played football, the idea was just to tackle the runner, intercept a pass when possible, fall on a fumble, and in a burst of good fortune, make a touchdown. But that was it; the game just continued.

Today I notice that when a player tackles a runner, or blocks a pass, he immediately leaps to an open area and does a dance. It involves whirling in a circle so his name is visible from all sides, while waving his arms for attention. The performance ends with a few gigantic jetés, albeit in football shoes. Then before play is resumed all the other players trot past him, slapping his palms and giving bear hugs.

A touchdown sets off a major production. Players form a chorus line, or a large circle, and do something between a hula and a ballet. This is preceded by a solo performance by the touchdown-maker, who symbolizes his success through interpretive body oscillation, much like a première danseuse.

There are no extra points given for this performance, as far as I know, though it may have compensation in the size of the salary.

The other special performance featured is a game-long video of the head coach making faces that express his emotional involvement in the plays. Oscar nominations, as yet, do not include this category, but it may eventually come.

So my viewing of the Super Bowl was minimal. My attention was taken by the dancing players and the close-ups of the coaches.

I missed most of the actual game.

CALL IT PROGRESS

NO HUMANS NEED APPLY

It seems we have some good news and some bad news.

Government spokesmen aver that the high rate of unemployment is bottoming out and that very soon employment will be on the rise again. This is the good news.

The bad news is, the new jobs will go to robots.

So far, Japan has put over 10,000 robots to work. They have what they call full robot employment. It is true that some of the older robots are out of work, but things are looking up for the young, second-generation robot. Up until now, the older generation were nothing more than a series of ball and socket joints screwed to the floor that turned out quotas of ball and socket joints.

Not so the new robots. These will come with senses of sight and hearing. They will even have a sense of touch, which implies a judgment as to the quality of their work, whether it be good or bad.

Also, they seem to be fast eliminating the old harangue about equal employment for women. In the case of most robots, sex discrimination engenders little controversy.

Things are getting tougher for unions, too. None of the new robots has joined up. They all seem to be right-to-work hardheads.

We have seen the movie "E.T." He is not a member of a union. He isn't even a citizen, which raises the additional question: is he an undocumented alien robot taking a job away from an American robot?

Complications seem endless. Computer-robots are already working in government employment offices, which could tilt new jobs away from normal people. Even the term "normal people" is becoming subject to criticism in factories where the number of employed robots exceed the number of people.

Without going too deeply into the ethics of deception, there is one other solution to the people-unemployment problem being evidenced. Many of those looking for work have been attaching levers and buttons to themselves when applying for a job, with remarkable success.

WHO SAID THAT?

Has a machine spoken to you lately?

Our first experience was some while ago when a trash can said, "Thanks for not littering," in a tinny falsetto voice. At least we think that is what it said. It was late in the day, the trash can was tired, and its lid squeaked.

Now more things have started talking. It is bad enough when you go through a toll booth and the coin box growls "Thank you" after you throw quarters into it, but talking soft drink machines are really the pits.

The whole idea of standing there, listening to what a slightly rusty bottle-dispenser has to say, is revolting in the extreme.

In fact, it's insulting. The machine expects you to pay strict attention while it talks, but it has no intention of listening to you in return. In fact if you try putting in a word or two it will very likely shut you up by interrupting you.

One thing these dispensers say is, "Make your selection, please!" As if you were too stupid to know why you came to the machine in the first place.

And after it speaks it stands there burping and gurgling with refrigerator noises, waiting for you to do what it told you.

Furthermore, it pays no attention to your answer, which might be: "This is a lousy selection" or "Where can I get an old-fashioned Nehi?"

Notice it uses the word "please," which is a travesty in language. Please is supposed to mean "If you wish." But in this case if you don't do what the machine says you lose your money.

We understand that this horror is going to go on in several different languages besides English; namely, French, German, Spanish, and (you guessed it) Japanese.

What we expect the next machine to say to us is: "Hi, sucker. You are paying too much for your drink if you continue to support all this overhead."

The end is not yet in sight. Other gadgets are in the planning stages. But we hereby give fair warning to talking drink machines. We will stand for just so much nonsense from robots which take our money. Cross us up in any way, withholding either drink or money, and you are going to get the same resounding thump we used to give your old-fashioned, illiterate ancestors.

DO WE NEED PEOPLE?

Once in a while my world becomes completely unglued. At such a moment I realize there is another world at work, undoing the traditional world I had become accustomed to.

This happened to me when a young son of a friend of mine didn't know there were live bank tellers. You see, his family, when they wanted to deposit or withdraw money, went to the wall of a supermarket in which a computer was embedded. My friend inserted his bank card in a slot and the computer, which had the word "teller" inscribed on it, said, "Thank you. Please push your code number." Eventually the money came out and the thin, metallic void said, "Thank you. Transaction completed." My friend's son had never seen any person associated with the word "teller."

If it is the intent of our new world to do away with people, I think it is too bad.

You can now call an airline reservation number and a computer on the other end tells you what to do. You push phone buttons indicating where you want to fly and when, what airport you are departing from, and how many tickets you want. Then you hang up. Your reservation has been made automatically.

When I am on an airplane these days I don't dare ask if there is a *person* flying it. Suppose the flight attendant smiled and said, "No, of course not." Anyway, when one gets to his destination he gets on a train which is run by a computer and not a person. A computer voice tells him to get on when the doors open and to get out at the other end.

Even the hotel he arrives at can give him a room without involving a human desk clerk.

One walks over to a wall where there are slots and buttons and he inserts his credit card. Information is forthcoming as to what kind of rooms are available. All he does is push a button for his selection and a key comes out.

I sometimes go to a restaurant where I pay a certain amount of money and then go and select my food off a revolving turntable.

It seems a world is developing in which everyone is expendable except the customer. No one is a worker. I rather liked the old world I once lived in, where someone waited on me. I suspect "service" jobs, in the old-fashioned sense of the term, are somehow thought to be undemocratic.

Still, it isn't such a great example of equality when anyone can be replaced by a button.

TODAY'S BOOKS AND LIBRARIES

NEW BOOKS ARE POURING INTO THE LIBRARY OF CONGRESS AT THE RATE OF 7,000 A DAY. THAT IS WORSE THAN RAISING RABBITS

Books and libraries supposedly go together. They don't make songs about it, like "love and marriage go together like a horse and carriage," because it isn't easy to rhyme anything with library. Certain things just have a tradition of going together. "Apple pie without the cheese is like a kiss without the squeeze." It is firmly fixed in traditional thinking: You can't have a library without books.

The Library of Congress isn't so sure anymore.

Books multiply faster than libraries, but they don't last as long. Everyone has suspected this. We all know books in a bookstore begin falling apart as soon as you look inside the cover for the price.

It is the same in a library. Libraries in the United States are all built like big bunkers on the Maginot line and will last in their present state through the 21st century. But books, like the Hardy Boys series, will be lying there waiting to be taken out by the vacuum cleaner. Unhardy specimens, becoming unglued like some of the librarians facing this dilemma.

The cause of people, as well as books, becoming unglued is that new books are pouring into the Library of Congress at the rate of 7,000 a day. That is worse than raising rabbits. Some place must be found to stack these books, let alone read them, so for every librarian the library probably has three bookcase builders.

Books wear out faster if they are read than if they are not read. So one solution would be to publish more books no one wants to read. A lot is being done in this direction.

But not reading books is not the logical solution, so in order to avoid becoming the world's largest brick garbage can, the Library of Congress has resorted to transferring books onto steel disks, which are indestructible and can store the equivalent of 300 books in a space one-sixteenth of an inch thick. Pictures and all.

We don't want to know how this is done. It has something to do with microscopic, optical laser technology, which is best left to science-fiction writers. And the whole idea terrifies anyone who likes to read in bed.

What the projecting of laser-beam books on screens will do to all our gentle, soft-spoken librarians is difficult to say. Evidently they are all going to be laser technicians with engineering degrees and come from MIT, instead of those nice ivy-covered, upstate teacher's colleges with Alma Mater.

Worst of all, it will mean an end to the bookmark, the only inexpensive gift left to buy in the world today.

MEDIA MADNESS

COMMERCIAL RELIEF

Many people think that television has not only hit a new low but that it somehow bears responsibility for society's ills. It could be true, considering the kind of programs we have to select from day after day and night after night.

Still, the situation isn't all bad.

We have finally found a solution to the poor TV quality by leaving the room to visit the refrigerator during the featured show and returning in time for the ads. Television seems much better since we changed our viewing habits. The new system has another advantage in that it gives more time to sort out the snacks and pour the drinks, whereas before it was always a rush.

Watching only ads is less stressful and gives one more hope. The feature programs usually deal with a woman whose husband and child have been kidnapped or done away with; an airplane about to blow up; dope addicts; officials of justice taking bribes; and so on and on.

But the ads are different. They promise us a better life.

The commercials gently explain that we can easily cope with the misfortunes vividly exploited on the featured programs if we simply buy the right product. It is all demonstrated before our very eyes. Troubles depart when we use the right shampoo. We can avoid financial disaster by staying calm and dry with the right deodorant.

Even better, we can win the spouse of our choice by offering the proper stick of gum or breath mint. Your boss will be delighted to have you share the same car or elevator if you have showered with the soap that makes you clean and fresh. Good things, beyond number, can be yours if you only gargle with a special mouthwash or soak your hands in a mild dishwashing liquid.

Even "educational" television is worrisome. The very symbol of instability, they're always just about to go off the air because you haven't sent in your pledge. This symptom, known as viewer's guilt complex, is responsible for more problems than we can imagine.

Commercials have better music and friendlier dialogue. Everyone comes out a winner. The only villains are ants and cockroaches who get done in by a walking-talking can of poison. Your safe future is not only assured, it is reassured. Who can doubt the wholesome verity of any statement on any product spoken to you by that epitome of grandfatherly wisdom, John Houseman?

If you find you are getting more and more disgusted with the programs on TV, try the commercials.

ALL-DAY BREAKFAST

It is time Americans woke up. It is not communism that is taking over the United States, it is cereal companies.

Americans have become so manipulated by the cereal interests that a bacon-and-egg breakfast has become lost to our culture. It exists only in strange mutated forms under such frightening names as "Egg McMuffin" and "Croissanwich."

Cereal ads imply there is no other reasonable way to get nourishment. One ad shows a person—representing *you*—eating a bowl of cereal. An ominous, superimposed voice asks if you are satisfied with your choice. You smugly say you are. Then the voice gloats over you: "Ha, ha, you will have to eat *12 bowls* of your cereal to equal the vitamins contained in *one bowl* of Vita-chew, which furnishes vitamins for the whole day!"

This is complete nonsense. What are you going to do for the rest of the day, anyway? Sit around dreaming of beef stew? Why do you have to eat an entire day's nourishment in one bowl?

Not much is said in the way of flavor. Everything is crunch! This is because cereal has no flavor, except perhaps to a horse or cow. People have eaten portions of the box without knowing the difference. Cereal companies are aware of this, so you never see people on television eating plain cereal. It always has other things in it like strawberries, bananas, raisins, or even nuts and dates. You have to pretend it's the cereal underneath that you're eating.

The ads show how you must eat the stuff—always with reckless gusto or even sloppy abandon. This is apparently the way healthy people eat. Well, it is not so much eaten as slobbered, with milk running down from the lips, or dripping from the chin.

Cereal boxes once had a small section in a grocery store. Now they have complete aisles of endless display. It frightens me. Now I've spoken out, you readers may never hear of me again.

The cereal Mafia may have struck.

SAVE OUR BILLBOARDS!

Rumor has it that Oregon is not crowded with tourist traffic. Studies are being made to correct this situation.

The main reason hordes of people are not jamming Oregon roads is that the state has no billboards. There are vast areas with nothing to look at. The modern tourist cannot be expected to travel any distance exposed to frightening expanses of what might be described as raw scenery. Many have not seen it before and of course feel threatened.

Tourists will drive miles to anywhere as long as a road is protected from unsightly wooded hillsides by continuous lines of billboards, reassuring the traveler that he is in no danger of leaving civilization. Preferably the signs should be about the standardized comforts ahead, such as motels, fast-food houses, and stores selling cheap candy and souvenirs.

This is one reason that places like Florida, southern California, and even Cape Cod are so popular. They have no scenery left to spoil the view. Everything is filled in and paved over, leaving no ugly contours caused by trees, hills, or bays.

Also, Oregon is blemished by what can be described as "natural" shoreline. This is land that consists of grass, trees, and beaches going right down to the ocean. It means that tourists have nothing to look at except plain, ordinary water, sand, and misshapen rock formations.

Florida has wisely corrected all this and hidden the water from view by building huge condominiums in front of it, thus presenting an unending panorama of pink stucco, nighttime orange and blue lighting arrangements, and large parking lots painted with interesting diagonal white lines. The parking lots are believed to hold the greatest attraction for tourists.

What Oregon can do at this late date to hide its unsightly natural scenery is not immediately apparent. Usually cutting down the trees and bulldozing the land for commercial construction is a starting point.

Tourists stand ready just outside the Oregon border, waiting, one might say, for the high sign.

REFLECTIONS OF A FUTURE MILLIONAIRE

"Pay Guernsey Le Pelley one million dollars."

The envelope came in my mail only last week, but I suppose I'll have to wait awhile for the money. I understand these things take time and they are not likely to send me the money right off.

Jealous friends tell me my chances of getting this million dollars are only half as good as getting struck by lightning at the North Pole, but what do they know? They didn't get an envelope.

In much lesser type it did say that one of the numbers below had to be a grand prize winner before they put the money in the mail, but this seems like only a formality. Meanwhile, I can get smaller things while I'm waiting, like an alarm clock telephone, so the time won't be completely wasted.

Another recent envelope offered $500,000. It is hard to pay attention to smaller offers, but I haven't thrown it away yet. The trouble is, I get a lot of $25,000 ones. It takes a long time to get to a million in only $25,000 chunks, so I'm tempted not to waste my time with them.

When one gets an envelope with an offer of a million dollars written across it in half-inch boldface type, it has a certain sobering effect. I admit it's hard not to hang around the front door waiting for the mailman each day, even though he seems totally unconcerned as to what is about to happen to me. Boy, I can't wait to see his face. Suppose they send the money in cash.

Just for the record, I want all my friends to know that having a million dollars won't make any difference in our relationship. Maybe I'll eat at a better restaurant once in a while, but that's all. They have this prime rib dinner advertised over on the trail for $14.95 and I might give it a try. I've been reading the ad for about six months.

Many years ago I had an acquaintance who received a sum of money anonymously. It wasn't a million, but who's counting? Anyway, it gave him a lot of problems, because he did nothing but worry and wonder who it was who sent it. I think he never fully trusted that he had it and thought that one day he would have to give it back.

I don't think I'm like that. With my million I'll go have my prime rib dinner and maybe even leave a $3 tip.

AND SO ON

EGGS AND EELS: THE ODD MAN OUT

In the course of one's earthly experience, a person acquires many odd friends and acquaintances. I don't mean odd in the sense of how they look, but just that they are "different." In my book that's the only way to define oddity.

Back in my boyhood years I had a friend who was odd. Kooky was the term I think we used then. While the rest of us were planning on becoming bankers, lawyers, engineers, or even cartoonists, he planned to go into the fishworm business. That may not strike some readers as odd. One does see signs, "Fishworms 4 sale." There are even ads in magazines for fish bait of different kinds, so there must be some normality about it. I won't quibble. But think about it. You might be at a gathering where someone says he is in oil, another in lumber or plastics. But how many say they are in fishworms?

Another friend, whom I won't name because he might read this, is a rainfall freak. Only he calls it precipitation. If I mentioned to him that I got a fan letter from Moline, Ill., he would nod respectfully—then in a moment: "Moline has a total annual precipitation of 39.39 inches." He might add: "The record for precipitation is Mt. Waialeale, Hawaii, with average rainfall of 460 inches." It's a nice piece of information. Especially if one is cornered at a convention of meteorologists.

But the fellow who really takes my oddity prize was an acquaintance I occasionally rode with on the bus. Our conversation started when a lady got on with a few groceries and dropped her eggs. The damage to the box of eggs I think was minimal, but the incident marked me for years to come.

My new friend whispered to me, "Psst, do you know how far you can drop an egg without breaking it?" Now, every egg I ever dropped, even from four inches, broke immediately, so I only looked at him.

"The record height a fresh egg was dropped without breaking was 650 feet." By the time I got off the bus I knew how many cars went across the George Washington Bridge in a day and how far every tall building swayed in the wind.

After several encounters I would brace myself for such bits of information as: "The amount of fish caught in Prince Edward Island in 1983 was 40,424 tons." Gradually I tried to avoid him.

The last time I sat with him—there was only one seat left on the bus—he unfolded to me that a certain Peter Dowdeswell had eaten a record number of 1,300 eels at one sitting. It was a hot day. I got off the bus early and walked the remaining five blocks.

LOST: ONE PRINCE; ONE WHITE HORSE

MAYBE ROMANCE WILL COME AROUND AGAIN, LIKE RIDING RAILROAD TRAINS

Just a few weeks ago I went to see a production of "The Student Prince." It seems that no one under age 40 had ever heard of it.

The music was wonderful. Sigmund Romberg melodies echoed in the lobby as people hummed their way back to their Cadillacs. But something was wrong. It was like strawberry shortcake on a bran muffin.

No one in the audience knew what the words meant. That was because the actors didn't, either. When the Prince held Kathie's hand in the garden, he didn't miss any lines, but the message sounded like reciting a recipe for Wiener schnitzel. The scene gave off all the compelling charm of mashed potatoes after three days in the refrigerator. Sure, the Prince promised faithfully to come back, but no one tingled at the thought.

Since then I have discovered the problem. The dialogue was written when people knew about romance. Actors and audiences communicated because romance was something one breathed, like air. But romance, as a viable commodity, apparently disappeared unnoticed in, or around, the early 1960s. It was displaced by graphic physicality, which required less art.

If there could be such a thing as a portrayal of serenading a girl under her window in today's videotape world, it would evolve as a screaming contest between a vocalist wearing a bright, neon yellow and pink striped, jewel-studded sweat shirt and an electronic sound track. He would probably have purple porcupine hair and would indicate the words had meaning by giving off frenzied, jerky gyrations around a huge guitar.

"Deep in my heart, dear . . ." may have meaning now only in that great cornfield in the sky.

In today's transplant world there is a vacuum where heartfelt things once existed. How could people look at each other and feel togetherness uncemented by a boy-girl wrestling match?

Maybe romance will come around again, like riding railroad trains. Or maybe it will only be historically recorded by college courses in "Romantic-speak," in which professors will learnedly explain how thoughts were once conveyed by a fanciful extension of word-meaning into feelings of rapture.

WOULD YOU BUY A USED PLAR FROM AN ASTRONOMER?

Players down at our town's free tennis courts have a short attention span. They have stopped discussing taxes and are now talking about a planet someone discovered outside the solar system.

Astronomers are on the verge of giving themselves a bad name. After a lot of this discovery ballyhoo, we learn that what they call a planet is made of gas. Hot gas, at that. Ten times hotter, they say, than Jupiter. That must mean Jupiter is all hot gas, too. Now to the average person this sounds like deception.

COMPARED WITH THOSE "SELLERS" OF GAS PLANETS, OLD-TIME FLORIDA REAL ESTATE OPERATORS WERE CHURCH DEACONS

Anyone who watched the 1969 moon landing has a right to believe a planet is something you can walk on. Compared with those "sellers" of gas planets, old-time Florida real estate operators were church deacons. Maybe they sold lots in Florida that no one could walk on, but at least you could paddle around on them in a rubber raft. Anyway, they weren't gas.

Some of these gas-planet astronomers try to explain that this new mass-of-gas discovery has to be called a planet because it isn't hot enough to be called a star. Well, the profession simply needs another name for this round, gassy nothing. The word has to be between planet and star. Something like "plar," which has a very honest sound to it.

Actually, we ought to take the double-talk out of a lot of professions. They do that just to make you say, "Please put that in language we can understand."

Maybe scientific conversations are not intended to be absolutely honest in the first place. Esoteric words, even pig Latin, can make one feel slightly superior.

Or maybe, in the case of astronomers, the science-fiction writers are making them feel obsolete. They are fighting back.

DEVIL'S FOOD FOR THOUGHT

According to recent surveys reported in newspapers, not very many people believe in hell anymore.

My interest in this subject is not because I think any great effort should be made on behalf of hell. If hell can't hack it on its own, who am I to build a fire under it? And I don't think it is worthwhile to try to restore hell to its former place as the main environmental hazard in the eternal landscape. I just want to know what happened to it.

Many church leaders are concerned with hell's obvious decline as a second choice. Presumably, in the old days a lot of people went to church just as much to steer themselves away from the horrible possibility of hell as they did to get a ticket to heaven. But sermons, according to several sources, have stopped mentioning hell.

I remember, as a child, that the kids in my neighborhood were very much aware of the grisly images of hell as a possible future prospect. They didn't plan going there themselves, but they had a confident suspicion that half their playmates would wind up getting their britches burned.

There was a Gallup poll taken which revealed even then that 71 percent believed in an "afterlife" where they would live in an attractive, though thinly populated, place called heaven. But the poll also showed that only 1 percent felt that hell was any threat to anybody.

Probably what has happened is that there has been a transposition of meanings. In our modern world sin, which was what pushed one hellward, has become more or less legal. Well, not only legal but, if one is educated by television, necessary, if one hopes to lead a normal life of heavenly satisfaction.

So what have you got left on heaven's side? By reverse inference heaven begins to look like a house of hellish confinement, with nasty bars of moral restriction at every window, while hell is being presented as the place with harp music.

Certainly we should not try to restore hell. But we should be careful not to mistake it for heaven.

THE HONESTY POLICY

Is honesty still the best policy, or has it been repealed by the Supreme Court?

Recently a poll in the United States found that 94 percent of the people thought honesty was an "extremely important" quality to have in a friend. It showed up as about twice as important as any other quality. At the same time the poll indicated that only 8 percent thought President Reagan was always honest, which presumably indicates not many people think of Mr. Reagan as a real friend. Only 8 percent thought newspapers were always honest, so the press doesn't come out any better. But only 3 percent thought congressmen were always honest, so as far as honesty goes it looks as if we are all on our own, wandering in a moral wasteland.

More than half of those questioned thought people have become less honest in the past 10 years. The problem seems to be, nothing is actually right or wrong anymore. Truth has become a relative quality.

This was all brought home to me a few weeks ago when my battery went dead and my car wouldn't start.

When I finally got my car to the garage, the mechanic looked things over with the rather disdainful look of the professional and announced, "You need a new battery." Upon which I took a packet of official documents out of my glove compartment and handed them to him.

"The battery is only 18 months old," I said. "As you can see, it is guaranteed for five years."

Mr. Wrenchwell gave me a cold, knowing smile. "No battery lasts five years," he said. "We'll give you some credit toward a new one."

I still insisted. "I bought this battery because it was guaranteed to last five years!"

Another man spoke up. "You're lucky. My five-year battery lasted 11 months. It went dead when I was 500 miles away from home."

I went to the boss. "If a battery lasts only about a year, why not say so and guarantee it for a year? Why lie about it?"

"People think batteries guaranteed for only a year aren't very good," he explained, obviously fed up with me. "So they are guaranteed for five years!"

In the end I had to buy a new battery—with a five-year "guarantee" sealed in a cellophane packet.

IS NUTTY NORMAL?

Anyone who reads newspapers or watches television knows by now that we live in a weird world. We all get so accustomed to absurdity that it passes for normality.

A moose is in love with a cow in Shrewsbury, Vt. They have been making cow-eyes and moose-eyes at each other for some time now.

Whales beach themselves on Cape Cod and California shores for some unfathomable reason. People then rush down to the seaside and try to push them back into the water. I suppose this will eventually develop into a game called whale-pushing. No accurate score can be kept, because many suspect that the whales who get pushed back sneak around and beach themselves in a new spot.

And of all things, the American Civil Liberties Union is making an effort to wipe out the last vestige of religion from public life in America even though this would baffle the Pilgrims and the framers of the Constitution. But obviously, one can't have cities around with names like San Diego and St. Paul. Heaven forbid. Changing the name of San Francisco to Hillsville has already been suggested.

The Treasury Department has announced that the United States has managed to build the largest public and private debt in the nation's history. This is accepted in a sort of gleeful wonderment, like a baseball player hitting a record number of home runs. There is also the Department of Agriculture, which reveals that America—the breadbasket of the world—now buys more farm products from foreign countries than it sells abroad.

It seems that one can buy two cats from Neiman-Marcus for $2,800. The price is evidently determined by the fact that they have designer spots, even though a cat is a cat. The Humane Society is properly horrified and suggests something like burning one's charge card.

Then there is the White House! President Reagan had a number of underlings who were running US foreign policy, selling arms to Iran, giving millions to the contras, right under his nose and not even telling him about it. Whillikers, the President must have had one big surprise when they told him what was going on.

Well, that's the way it is. Strange things keep happening, but they seem more and more normal.

THE TRUE GOOSE BUMP

For several days I have taken to researching a problem of which very little is known—the study of goose bumps.

Goose bumps are also known as goose pimples, or by the more vulgar term goose flesh. For the more sensitive reader I have coined the Latin phrase *Anser papula*. Since no scientific records have been compiled, I think it is time someone took this seriously.

I HAVE NEVER WITNESSED A BRIDE WALKING DOWN THE AISLE COVERED IN GOOSE BUMPS, THOUGH I HAVE OFTEN SEEN A GROOM COVERED WITH PERSPIRATION

It should be made clear that this study does not include, as some might imagine, the goose. A goose *may* have goose bumps, but geese do not identify with the human social concept of the term. So bumps on geese are outside the perimeter of this discussion.

Also, this study does not include so-called false goose bumps, or *Anser papula falsa*, which occur when one is caught in 38 degree weather dressed in summer cotton. We are concerned here with only the true goose bumps (*Anser papula vera*), which occur when one is alone in the house and hears a shutter bang, or sees shapes looming along a dark, lonely road.

A survey revealed that more women than men get goose bumps. Taking into consideration that men are inclined to lie about their goose bumps, we have to assume a 15 percent margin of error. The results show that 85 percent of females admit to getting goose bumps, as opposed to 58 percent for males. The breakdown for males was conventional; 26 percent maintained they had never had a goose bump, 14 percent had no opinion, and 2 percent didn't know what a goose bump was.

Of the total women confessing to true goose bumps, almost half said the cause was not shutters bumping in the night, but monster movies on television, while many said they got goose bumps just before their wedding.

Thus far, I have never witnessed a bride walking down the aisle covered in goose bumps, though I have often seen a groom covered with perspiration, so I confess this study is not complete in every way.

Once I have brought the goose bump study to a satisfactory conclusion, I intend to take up butterflies in the stomach. Or *Papilio stomacha.*

LOCKER DEMOCRACY

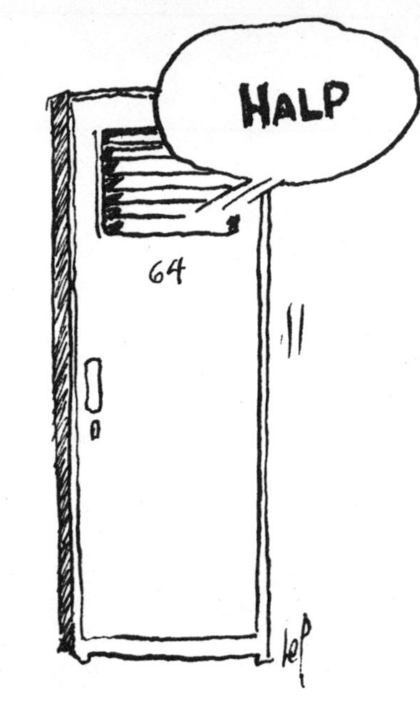

There has been some slightly dopey controversy about a school principal searching students for dope.

The fact that such traditional and necessary procedure could flummox good citizens of a democracy and go all the way to the Supreme Court of the United States for a solution leaves all us old-timers down at the town tennis courts bug-eyed.

Somehow the idea has gotten around in the childworld that a school is a microcosm of a democracy and that the teen-age population thereof controls the officials by reason of the Constitution. Exploitation of such a pseudo legalism is what gives lawyers their low trust-rating with the public.

When we went to school occasional searches, especially of lockers, were an accepted necessity. After all, lockers were a convenience furnished by the school, and looking into them had a very practical side. Strange smells sometimes floated out of them. Old sweat shirts, athletic socks, and sneakers often accumulated in the bottom. Occasionally someone's bag lunch containing sardine sandwiches would remain for a week or more. In one case, a sophomore accidentally left a cat inside for several days when she went off to compete in a regional debate with the team.

Certainly, the Constitution protects children. Good heavens, something has to. But the search and discipline of children are part of their protection. Anyone in the parent category knows this. Children do not spring full grown from the head of Zeus, as Venus did, contrary to their egocentric opinion of their maturity level. For instance, the constitutional right to bear arms can hardly extend as low as high school freshmen.

In bygone days, arguments about searching did not involve switch blades, guns, or drugs, but ponies. A pony was a condensed version of literature, history, or whatever, and it was frowned upon by those entrusted with education. If a student wanted the education of reading "Moby Dick," he was supposed to read it, even though to some this may seem a highly reactionary idea.

But now, with drugs and firearms being allowed into the picture, mostly through relinquishing supervision, one has to wonder what is happening to the children. What do they need?

They need protection more than full equality.

Equality comes later, with responsibility.

ARAFAT BEARDED

MR. ARAFAT WOULD HAVE HAD MORE SUCCESS AS A PR MAN IF HE REMEMBERED TO SHAVE

Great leaders usually understand one can compromise on a deal here and there without losing the whole farm.

Maybe if Yasser Arafat had cashed in on Camp David he could have laughed all the way to the West Bank. His friendly smile kept saying "yes yes" but his lips said "no no."

Yasser, meaning "no sir," has put the Fatah in the fire.

All of the news media quarterbacks called the signals as to what went wrong. Mr. Arafat would have had more success as a PR man if he remembered to shave. Maybe he does shave, but he uses the electric razor that doesn't shave as close as a blade. And he may not even know about safety razors. "Safety" to him refers to something he has to turn on when his pistols are tucked inside his belt.

Consideration should always be given to the theory that Arafat's beard stubble is carefully cultivated to make him look more like a terrorist. Then too, the continuous unshaven look gives the impression that the Mideast is frozen in time. Everyone keeps on waiting for the man to shave, or else grow a beard. When the whiskers don't get any longer or shorter everyone thinks it is still the same day.

Quite likely Arafat started out to grow a long beard like Ayatollah Khomeini but he decided he wasn't tall enough.

With all his faults, Arafat is a moderate but he could be the only person in the Middle East who has a sense of humor. If Arafat goes, the PLO will move closer to the influence of Damascus, where there is no sense of humor whatsoever.

Damascus is the capital of Syrious.

WHAT GOES UP . . .

One of the few things I learned in school which I felt I could depend upon through the years was the law of gravity. Now, I find, they want to change it.

If one can't believe in Newton, Galileo, and Einstein anymore, where can one turn for wisdom? Dan Rather? Bill Buckley? The Jackson Five? There are so few things one can feel secure about today that they ought to leave the law of gravity alone.

I remember so well my grammar school class when these wonders of physics were first revealed to me. An apple fell out of a tree, I read, and hit Isaac Newton on the head. "Ouch," said Isaac Newton. Picking up the apple, he regarded it. "Why did not the apple fall upwards?" Well, we know the answer. He decided it was because of the law of gravity. The gravitation of the earth pulled things toward it.

There were things about the law of gravity which gave me a few secret doubts. That was because Galileo mucked things up, throwing stuff off the Leaning Tower of Pisa to prove everything dropped at the same rate of speed. I always maintain that a penny would fall to earth at the same rate of speed as a 10-ton truck, but only because of my respect for education.

Things have gone topsy-turvy now. The law of gravity has been technically repealed. Newspapers are reporting new laws of "hypercharge" and "electromagnetism." They are monkey wrenches thrown into gravity's finely geared machinery. No longer do things fall to earth at exactly the same speed.

Since the 16th century, the law of gravity has been working perfectly. And I learned as a boy the words of wisdom pronounced to me by an old mechanic: "If it ain't broke, don't fix it." We have gotten along without hypercharge so far, so who needs it?

It has been a great balm of reassurance for me to see apples still falling out of trees in the prescribed manner, and I am ever so grateful for the truism "What goes up must come down," even though some of my tennis lobs tend to challenge it.

APPENDIX

RUN DATE	TITLE
08-16-88	A bird's- and a frog's-eye view
08-30-88	A chowder of cats, a knot of toads . . .
06-13-83	A penny a pig, too
02-02-88	Abominable snowmen
04-16-86	All-day breakfast
12-05-83	Arafat bearded
06-28-88	Are the candidates real timber?
09-20-83	baby circuit, The
03-26-87	Bug off
04-18-84	Bumps in the Atlantic
06-23-87	Canned in the service
01-23-85	Cleats and tutus: super performances
05-04-82	Commercial relief
04-30-86	'Comrade, one of our freight trains is missing'
06-04-86	Devil's food for thought
12-03-86	Do we need people?
02-13-86	Draining Britain
01-09-06	Eggs and eels: the odd man out
09-16-86	Fred the sofa
06-12-89	Friendly mosquitoes
03-25-83	From one geezer to another
03-03-82	Gassing game
06-16-87	Glasnost in the air
07-26-88	Going to the dogs
10-31-85	Good guys get the beeps
03-06-86	Great and near great

RUN DATE	TITLE
10-12-82	Gridirony
05-17-82	Grin-and-bear policy
10-06-83	Heroes and turkeys
03-10-87	honesty policy, The
05-12-87	Hot hands, cold feet
02-03-87	I ain't a prude, but . . .
03-03-87	I ain't a prude, Part 2
12-16-86	Is nutty normal?
08-11-87	It's an enigma
07-21-83	Kangaroo cute
07-15-86	Layers of delight
02-02-83	Letting things lean
10-31-83	Life-size presidents
02-07-85	Locker democracy
03-22-85	Lost: one prince; one white horse
02-22-83	Martin Van who?
10-06-87	Milkmen of yesteryear
04-07-87	Modern-day dinosaurs
02-02-84	Moon over Moscow
05-15-85	Mythical creatures: unicorns and Busybodies
08-26-82	No humans need apply
05-12-83	No newts is good newts
11-01-88	No speka da English
06-11-82	Oink!
08-09-84	old Giza, The
02-24-89	paws population, The
08-09-88	presidency: appearance is everything, The
10-06-88	Presidents with vices
12-31-82	Raccoonteur
12-01-82	Reagan bust, The
04-11-86	Reflections of a future millionaire

RUN DATE	TITLE
10-30-85	Save our billboards!
04-13-82	Save Venus
10-20-83	Skyjack to Cuba
05-24-88	smell of youth, The
03-25-86	Smiley 'gators
03-03-89	Sweet insincerity
10-28-86	terrific paleolithic, The
09-23-83	Today's books and libraries
07-22-85	Trials of travel
08-11-85	true goose bump, The
05-10-88	unhuggable black rhino, The
07-01-85	What goes down . . .
02-28-86	What goes up . . .
09-01-82	Who said that?
01-03-85	Would you buy a used plar from an astronomer?